Web Business Success

The Entrepreneur's Guide to Web Sites That Work

Susan C Daffron & James H. Byrd

Logical Expressions, Inc.
http://www.logicalexpressions.com

ISBN-13: 978-0-9749245-0-2

ISBN-10: 0-9749245-0-4

Library of Congress Control Number: 2006909228

Contents

Introduction

Going Online

As Web developers, for years we have heard people say longingly, "I want to start an online business, so I can quit my crummy job and work from home." Or business owners will tell us that they plan to put up a Web site "when they have time."

Of course inertia being what it is, most of them have done nothing at all. Or if they have done something about getting their online business started, they spent a whole lot of money on "get rich quick" schemes that didn't pay off.

Let's face it: if you were planning to become a pig farmer, it makes sense to learn something about pigs before you start. Yet people seem to think that it's different with the Internet. They think you can just pay someone to put up a Web site and suddenly untold riches appear.

The reality couldn't be further from the truth.

We wrote this book to cut through the hype that surrounds almost everything online these days. Creating a Web business is no different than any other business: it requires work. However, because you are operating "virtually," it means you can live more or less wherever you want. You can work from home or conduct business from the coffee shop on the corner.

Because we have operated our business largely online since 1994, we have been able to move to a remote part of Idaho. Not everyone may want to do that, but thanks to the Internet, we've been able to realize our dream of living where we want, far away from "the big city." We earn a decent living from our Web sites and online ventures. It's not impossible.

If you're interested in taking your bricks-and-mortar business online or in starting an online business and becoming a "Webpreneur," this book gives you the information you need to make good choices in your new venture.

Freedom vs. Security

If you are thinking of starting an online business, or any business for that matter, you need to take a hard look at yourself. As noted, we love the freedom of working from our home in the trees. But this lifestyle is not for everyone.

If you think running your own business means you can just work in your pajamas and have lots of flexibility, you're only seeing part of the picture. Flexibility is great. Freedom from the 9-to-5 cubicle-dweller existence means you can pick up your kids after school and avoid the commute. You can enjoy your family, hobbies, and your life outside of work.

Self-employment does have downsides as well.

1. Lack of a steady paycheck. It should be obvious, but some people fail to realize that until you have customers, you aren't making money. An online business takes some time to ramp up. Be prepared.

2. Loneliness. Many people need to be around other people and don't work well alone. If your friendships are mostly inside the office, when you start your own business, plan to join some organizations to get you out of the house and among people again, so you don't go nuts.

3. Self-discipline. Not everyone is self-motivated enough to work on their own. If you work from home, you have TV, kids, pets, the phone, the refrigerator, and endless busywork you can use as excuses to keep from actually getting work done. Even if your business is located in an office, you can still spend all day surfing the Internet to avoid real productive work. No boss is going to yell at you, but when you're self-employed doing no work means you make no money.

Even if you already have a business, you need to consider whether you have the time and the resources to take your business online. A Web site does not run itself. If your business is barely eking along and your systems don't work offline, rest assured, things will not improve when you add a Web presence into the mix.

When you have a Web site, you need to commit yourself to these things:

1. Answering email reliably and religiously. You need to follow up on any inquiries quickly. Many small businesses are lax in follow up. This type of poor customer service doesn't play well at all online. People are used to almost instant

gratification. Plus, most of us spend more time than we realize dealing with email. Even if you automate many of your customer communications, you must still react quickly when someone has a question or complaint about a product. Responses take time, so you must make time for it. You will soon lose your credibility (and sales) if it takes you a week to respond to email queries.

2. Committing yourself (or your staff) to education. Understanding how the Web works and learning best practices can help you spend your money wisely and avoid serious online mistakes that can hurt your business. (Buying this book is a step in the right direction!)

3. Creativity, moxie, and a willingness to sell. If you can't imagine selling anyone anything, you won't. If you love thinking up new marketing ideas and writing creative copy, your Web business will shine.

Decide What to Do and Avoid the Hype

Nothing happens without a plan. You've probably begun researching your options online. If you have read a bunch of hype from Internet "gurus," you now are probably completely confused. That dreck makes us insane.

Here's a little hint that will save you a whole lot of money. All those Internet marketing "gurus" go to the same conferences, write the same testimonials for each other, and have the exact same sales pages and Web sites. All they do is change the text a little. If you pay attention, you can spot them, and avoid them.

When you see a sales letter Web site with the same old white box on a blue background with red "important" text, scroll down to the bottom. You'll undoubtedly discover that the amazing product that will change your life is "only" $997 and it includes 150 hours of bonus footage of the same group of gurus telling each other how great they are.

These online marketing "techniques" all started with a couple of guys who could write great direct mail copy and transferred their knowledge to the Internet. Now they sell their "secrets" in these massive thousand dollar kits. Yet realistically, you can get much of the same information from an $11 book from Amazon.com or your public library. For example, if you go to Amazon and do a search on Dan Kennedy (one of the earliest marketing big wigs), you'll find his book, minus the hyped-up sales letter. Yes it's a good book. No, it doesn't cost $997.

So here's an Internet consumer tip. The next time you are falling for one of those sales letters with the same old white box on a blue background with red "important" text, just close the window. Go to Amazon and do a search. Save $986 and line your own pockets with it instead of someone else's. Use it to buy an entire library's worth of business books.

Now let's get beyond the hype. Basically, you can make money online in four ways:

1. Sell physical products (ecommerce or eBay)
2. Sell services (consulting, Web design, writing, and innumerable other services)
3. Sell advertising (Google AdSense or affiliate programs)
4. Sell monthly services (hosting or membership sites)

Most of the sites you see are some variation of these themes. It all depends on what you're good at and like to do.

In our business, we've actually experienced all four categories. Now we sell books and software, which fall into category 1. You see the term "infoproducts" online a lot. Don't be confused; it's still a physical product, so they still fall into category 1. We've sold writing, editing, Web design and programming services for years (category 2). Our online content sites have AdSense on them (category 3), and we sold a hosted product (category 4).

Web Business Reality Check

Okay, now that you've thought about what you might want to do, it's time for a bit of a reality check.

As noted, endless hype surrounds new technology in general and the Web in particular. It's sometimes difficult to remain grounded in business reality when you are always being sold a better, faster, more "amazing" solution.

So before you invest the time and energy to create a Web site, make sure you plot out and understand your own business model thoroughly. Start with a clear business plan. Develop concrete goals that are achievable. Be certain that you can find your customers and know what appeals to them. Once you have these business basics nailed down, you can create a Web site that supports your goals. You will also avoid many frustrating and costly mistakes.

Before we go any further, you must realize that a Web site is not magical. It will not save your business or make you a millionaire overnight. A Web site will not necessarily cost you less to operate than a bricks-and-mortar or mail order business. This caveat is especially true if your business grows beyond a size you can manage comfortably on your own.

Try to view your Web business as one more tool for marketing the products and services you provide. Make it a part of a larger business strategy. Don't expect it to be a substitute for quality products, honest salesmanship, and good customer service, and don't assume it will be a no-money-down project.

Treating Your Business Like a Business

One of the basic realities of going into business is treating your business like a business. If you are starting up an online business or adding a Web component to an existing business, you need to take into account the four areas of business operations:

- Legal - business licenses, contracts, trademarks, copyrights

- Finance - bookkeeping, accounting, taxes

- Marketing - sales, advertising, public relations, promotion

- Operations - manufacturing, shipping, business processes

Of the four, we could argue that marketing is the most important. You can put off getting a lawyer, and when you're just getting started before you have any sales, finance isn't a huge issue. Operations are generally refined into systems that develop with experience over time.

But until you start marketing and making sales, you have a hobby, not a business. When we started our business, we took an entrepreneurship course through the local adult education cooperative. In that course, the instructor had a mantra: "nothing happens until somebody sells something." It's true.

Myth vs. Reality

Before we get into the technical nitty-gritty, we'd like to spend a little time debunking a few myths. Over the past few years, we have spoken with a lot of clients who had unrealistic expectations about doing business on the Web. Here are a few misconceptions we've encountered:

Misconception #1: Technology somehow makes it easier to run a business.
That just isn't true. A Web business must solve the same problems as a bricks-and-mortar business. Yes, there are differences, but it's an open question as to whether those differences make doing business easier or harder!

Why? Because with a Web business, you still have all the same core business functions. All that has changed is your customer "interface." The Web changes the method you use for interacting with your customers. You still have marketing, operational, financial, and legal issues to resolve. These business realities never go away, no matter how much automation you employ.

If you are not technically inclined, an ecommerce Web site can actually become an obstacle between you and control of your business. In fact, the technology can make it more, not less, difficult to perform marketing functions, do order fulfillment, compute your return on investment, or collect sales tax. You simply must be prepared to learn how to do some new things if you want ecommerce to work for you.

Here are some of the basics that a responsible Web storeowner should understand:

- How to use shopping cart software to manage your product line and orders.

- How to put images on the Web, like simple digital photography and image editing.

- How online payment works behind the scenes, and how to answer questions about the security of your Web site.

- How to use a Web page authoring tool, or how to hire the right person to update your site for you.

- How to use your payment gateway software to manage credit card payments (if these functions are not integrated with your shopping cart software).

Misconception #2: Running a Web business is cheaper.
While that may be true of a garage-spun startup, you'll find that your overhead starts
to keep pace with a bricks-and-mortar business as soon as you add a few employees.

For an extreme example of this, look at Amazon.com. They've been in business for
many years and it took many, many of those years before they started making a profit.
It takes a lot of money to operate their business and they manage a massive inventory.
They also pay numerous employees, and they have an enormously complex Web
infrastructure that needs to be maintained 24/7.

The ideal business for the Web is small. It doesn't require a huge staff to maintain its
infrastructure and customer relations. It's best if it offers a unique product, or series
of products, that can be produced on demand, either by download or through some
third-party fulfillment company.

A unique product line is crucial. It is simply too difficult to compete against companies
like Wal-Mart on mass-market items. You will be fighting a price war, and your
shipping charges will eat up what little margin you salvage.

Producing your product on demand is best because you don't have your cash tied
up in inventory. This ideal Web-based business delivers an electronic payload, like
software. It gives you the most opportunities for automating your business. Your Web
site can handle everything from taking the order to accepting payment, delivering
the product, thanking the customer, and selling them new "back-end" products in the
future.

Of course, this "ideal" business model assumes that you produce what you sell. What
if you resell? Then you need to come up to speed fast on how to properly manage an
inventory.

Inventory management is actually much harder than it sounds, especially if you are a
one-person operation. To ship within the recommended 24 hours, you must have the
items on hand. (You can try letting the supplier drop-ship directly to your customer,
but resolving disputes in that scenario can be challenging.)

You must have enough items in inventory to satisfy orders, without tying up too much
of your money in inventory that may never sell. (Maintaining that balance can result in
manual hair loss!) Yet if you fail to exercise control over inventory, you will be at risk

for one of the most common causes of business failure during economic downturns, i.e., too much product and no buyers.

Misconception #3: ANY business can make sales online.
It would be nice if that were the case, but again, it's simply not true. Some types of businesses just don't translate well to the ecommerce paradigm.

If you sell services, especially personal or professional services, ask yourself these two fundamental questions:

- Would you search for your type of service on the Internet (as opposed to the phone book, local paper, or word of mouth)?

- Would you purchase your type of service on the Internet? In other words, would you actually hit a Buy Now button for your type of service, and then fill in your credit card information?

If the answer to either of those questions is "no," then think twice before you invest in complex ecommerce solutions. You might be better off with a three- or four-page Web site that simply explains what you do (for more on this topic, see Online Brochure Sites).

Misconception #4: Running a Web business takes less of your time.
Even though you won't spend time standing behind a counter waiting on customers, your Web business still requires hands-on maintenance. Like we said earlier, you must respond to email queries. You must process the orders you receive through your site. You must thank customers, and contact them periodically to offer them new products.

Even if you sell one simple physical product, you must prepare the item for shipping yourself. You must pack it carefully and deal with getting it safely to the shipper. I'll bet it takes you longer to do all that than it does for a clerk to put a counter customer's order into a bag and hand it to her!

And last but not least…

Misconception #5: Running a Web business should not be attempted by beginners.

After all this discussion, we don't want to sound like we're trying to discourage people from doing business on the Web. Like we said, our business has been largely Web-based since 1994.

Our goal is to make it clear that doing business on the Web is like any other business. It has its advantages, but it also has its drawbacks. Unless you have a strong desire to learn about the technology, work hard, and make adjustments as needed, you shouldn't try it. In fact, you shouldn't try any kind of business!

Before you spend many hours and dollars investing in a Web business, take a long, hard, realistic look at the issues. Understand your goals and weigh the odds. Armed with an understanding of the pros and cons, you improve your chances of success significantly.

Our Story

Now that we've explained how we earn money online, you might be wondering who we are and how we ended up writing this book.

Back in 1994, we were living in Southern California doing the standard yuppie thing. We both had reasonably good jobs, but they were unsatisfying, partly because neither of us fit the So Cal mold (we don't tan and we hate crowds). But we figured that as a programmer and tech writer, we really had to be in a big city to find a job.

We felt like we were on the slow track to nowhere, working for companies run by dishonest people (who probably should have been in jail...but that's a different story). Every day, like most people we made the 1.25-hour commute on the very scary freeways to our jobs since it seemed like the only thing to do.

To remain sane, we regularly took vacations to get away from the city. Both of us yearned for mountains and needed periodic "tree fixes" to de-stress. For us, being off in the trees is where we felt most at home. On one trip to Idyllwild, California, a tiny town in the San Jacinto Mountains, we were walking around amidst the trees letting them work their magic on us as we tried to forget about life down in the city. It was raining and as we walked along the residential streets, we noticed a few nice houses.

Really nice houses. Idyllwild has no business except tiny tourist shops and we knew from the ads we'd seen that real estate was extremely expensive. We were struck by the notion: what do these people DO that makes it possible to live up here? Then it dawned on us. We realized that some of those houses probably had a phone line connected to a modem.

And the light dawned.

Back then, the Web was new, but we realized then and there that telecommuting was the answer. If we ran our own business, we could live anywhere we wanted. We could leave Southern California with its smog, freeways, and "beautiful people." We could live anywhere. It was such a freeing thought; we couldn't get it out of our heads. We read every business book we could find and two months later, we formed Logical Expressions.

As with every business, you have to start somewhere. We wrote a business plan and Susan quit her job in January 1995 to run LE full time. At that time, we offered technical writing, design and editing services. In August, James quit his job and began doing contract-programming work. All of our clients were in Southern California, but we used email, fax, FedEx, and the occasional meetings to work with our clients. Because our clients were used to not dealing with us face-to-face, we realized that our dream of moving away from the Southland was within our grasp. So, we used our vacation time to explore various areas of the West with lots of trees and mountains. We found Sandpoint, Idaho on one of those journeys and fell in love with the Inland Northwest.

Our next project was selling our condo and getting ourselves and our business moved, which was no small task in a terrible real estate market. But again, we researched. We read everything we could about selling a house and sold our place in May of 1996. We bought an unfinished log home in Sandpoint and moved our cats and all our computer equipment to a tiny rental ski chalet on Schweitzer Mountain where we lived and worked while the house was finished. To our clients, the transition was virtually seamless with the exception of different telephone numbers.

As we became more involved in the community, we realized that we wanted to share some of our knowledge with people in the area. In Southern California, there was a successful and widely adored computer magazine that we both used to read. We thought that with our editorial and computing background, we could create a similar magazine.

We sold ads, wrote articles, and worked with pretty much everyone over the Internet. Our writers were (and are) all over the world. We put out the first issue of *Computor Companion* in the Fall of 1999. It was extremely well received and we heard from people in Spokane that they wanted it there too. So we expanded our distribution.

By July of 2001 after the dot-bomb crash, we ended up deciding not to print *Computor Companion* anymore. Even though readers continued to love it, our advertisers were folding or cutting their spending considerably. So *Computor Companion* lives on in the cyber-realm as an online magazine at http://www.computorcompanion.com. Advertising income now comes from Google, which is a heck of a lot easier than the old fashioned way of selling ads.

Our experience with the magazine had other great ripple effects as well. The first one was the Logical Web Publisher (LWP), which is the software that is behind all our large content sites. Using this tool, we can create these sites quickly and easily by just copying and pasting in articles.

After the success of *Computor Companion*, we used the LWP to set up ezine sites about our various interests. People liked our newspaper columns and since we owned the rights, we put them online. For years, we have been sending out ezines about computers, pets, and Sandpoint. All of them also have Google AdSense on them.

- Logical Tips - http://www.logicaltips.com

- Pet Tails - http://www.pet-tails.com

- Sandpoint Insider - http://www.sandpointinsider.com

Now as you can tell, we are expanding into book publishing. We released a book called *Vegan Success* (http://www.vegansuccess.com) and this one is our second book. Again these books are sold online through our sites, Amazon.com, and BN.com. Thanks to technology, we don't have to stock inventory. They are printed "on demand" when people order them.

Our sites have always used quality writing to draw in visitors. We have never engaged in any type of "black hat" unethical techniques. We believe that the Web is about information. Good content never goes out of style.

About this Book

This book came about because of classes we've taught, articles we've written and many, many conversations we've had with our Web site clients over the years.

Many of our clients and students had done research online and it left them hopelessly confused. The Web is huge and when you're just starting out, it's easy to become completely overwhelmed. We decided to write up all the advice and information we give our clients. The result is the book you are holding in your hands.

This book is divided up into a number of sections. Because this book is about the Internet, at the end of each section, you'll find a list of online resources you can visit for further information. These resources are generally ones we've used that have been around for a long time.

Here are the main sections of the book and what they contain:

Creating Your First Site
Virtually anything you do online requires a Web site, so the first section is about creating your first site. Within that section we get into the basics of Web design, content, and graphics. We also explain how to find a developer you can work with and go into some of the "extras" you can add to a Web site.

Getting Your Site Online
Once you have a site, you need a place to put it. This section goes through the ins and outs of domain names and hosting. It explains what you are getting for your money and how to find good, reliable companies.

Promoting Your Site
A Web site is useless if no one ever visits, so site promotion is a key element of Web business. This section goes into the ins and outs of search engines, optimization, linking and other ways you can get the word out about your site.

Creating an Ecommerce Site
If you ever plan to sell anything directly over the Web, you need to learn about ecommerce. This section explains the often-confusing world of merchant accounts, payment gateways, and shopping carts.

Business Operations and Practices
In the final section, we offer some final advice on how to keep your business running smoothly for the long haul.

At the back of the book, you'll also find a **Glossary** and an **Index** for reference.

Armed with this information, you can forge confidently into the world of your new Web business.

Start Up Resources

Here are a few Web resources with articles about starting a business:

- Entrepreneur Magazine - http://www.entrepreneur.com

- Inc. Magazine - http://www.inc.com/resources/startup/

- Small Business Administration - http://www.sba.gov/starting_business/

- Business Know How - http://www.businessknowhow.com

- Startup Journal (from the Wall Street Journal) - http://www.startupjournal.com/

- Service Corps of Retired Executives (SCORE) Free business counseling - http://www.score.org

Creating Your First Site

Getting Started

Before you do a Web site, it helps to understand what exactly a Web site is. Whether you create the site yourself or hire a Web developer, it helps to understand the process. Once you are familiar with the elements of a Web site, it's a lot easier to understand all the activities that are involved in getting a Web site onto the Internet.

Essentially, a Web site is basically just a series of documents that are all linked together and placed in a folder that is located on a server that is attached to the Internet. Web pages differ from other types of documents not necessarily because of the software used to create them, but because of the formatting language behind the scenes.

For example, you can create a text (.txt) file in Notepad, WordPad or even Microsoft Word. The format of the file is "plain text." Along the same lines, you can create a Web page in Adobe Dreamweaver or even Notepad, as long as the format is Hypertext Markup Language or HTML (.htm or .html). By putting special HTML codes into the page, a browser can read the file.

A Web site can be made up of one or many HTML files stored in a folder on a Web server. You add links into a Web page that connect it to other pages within your site or to any other page on the Internet. Adding photos and other graphics is actually just linking a picture into the HTML page. When you see Web pages with red x's or empty boxes where the pictures should be, it means that either the photo isn't on the server or the link is pointing to the wrong place.

Many problems with Web pages stem from poor file management. When you create a site, you need to pay attention to where files are, so you don't end up with broken links and missing pictures. We talk more about this subject and other design issues in the next section.

More on HTML

When you're creating a Web site, you'll hear the term HTML bandied about a lot, so it helps to know more or less how it works, at least in principle.

As we mentioned, HTML is actually a formatting language. You can use many tools to create an HTML page because basically it's quite simple. For example, every Windows computer has WordPad or Notepad on it. Hypertext Markup Language (HTML) is nothing more than a text file, which you can create in WordPad or Notepad. Within the text file are commands that are contained within angle brackets (greater than and less than signs), which are called tags. These tags are what tell the Web browser how to display the page.

Some HTML tags come in pairs, so there is a beginning and an ending tag. The end tag has a slash before the name. The displayed text of the page goes in between the formatting tags. Browsers ignore carriage returns in the text file, so you need to tell the browser where a new line starts either by using <P> paragraph tags or <BR> line break tags. For headings, you can use opening <H1> and closing </H1> heading tags. You can add smaller headings using higher numbered tags, such as <H2>, <H3>, and so on.

Obviously there are gazillions more tags and much, much more to know, but as you can see, HTML isn't rocket science. Web design tools just make the process of creating Web sites easier. Tools like Dreamweaver and FrontPage let you see what the page looks like while you are editing it. However, the Web design tool doesn't think for you, so you can easily make a huge mess if you never look at the HTML. (As Web designers, we've been tasked with redoing many, many bad pages created by people who obviously never looked at the code.)

If you decide to create the site yourself, you may want to download one of the free HTML editors available online, assuming you don't want to invest big money in Dreamweaver. The net result is the same: HTML pages. On the other hand, if you decide to contract with a Web developer, be very sure that they know HTML and not just the Web design tool.

Rome Wasn't Built in a Day

Now that you've thought about the business realities of the Web and know what a Web site is, it's time to think about creating your first Web site.

One thing that tends to lead people into the land of overwhelm is the sheer number of options you have when you create a Web site. It's time to take a deep breath and realize that you probably don't have the time and resources to implement them all.

Web sites tend to evolve over time. The natural evolution of many Web sites is:

- Stage One: You usually start off with an "online brochure" site. This site consists of static pages that explain your business (more on that in a moment).

- Stage Two: You add ecommerce features. In this stage, your customers can research your business and its offerings and conduct business with you over the Internet.

- Stage Three: You allow customers to engage with your site on a personal level. Perhaps you customize their browsing experience. Or you offer membership features that foster a sense of community.

But you have to start somewhere. If you get so overwhelmed by the options, you may not start at all.

Virtually any business needs to start with a Web site. It doesn't have to be an elaborate ecommerce site to begin with. In fact, it's better if it's not. First it's a good idea to get up to speed on issues relating to Web site design, content, and graphics. These elements are relevant to ANY Web site. Plus, if you are in a service business, you actually may never need an ecommerce site.

We often advise people to start with an online brochure site (Stage One). After they go through the development process and get it online, they then can learn and get used to the Web realities of answering email and paying attention to the Internet.

Now you may be asking: what's an online brochure site?

Online Brochure Sites

An online brochure site offers potential customers every piece of information they need to help them decide to hire you.

Your online brochure should describe all the benefits of your service and the types of problems you solve for your clients. A frequently asked questions (FAQ) page can help address common client concerns and objections. Testimonials from satisfied customers add enormous credibility. So do brief articles, Special Reports, or white papers authored by you, that show that you're an expert in your field.

The goal of your online brochure is the same as an offline one: to persuade your potential clients to call or email you so you can engage in person-to-person marketing and sales.

In general, if you must establish personal rapport and trust with your potential customers or clients, you will be much better off with a simple Web site that persuades rather than sells. Why even try to get prospects to pay online?

Instead, create a simple Web site that shows them why you are their best choice for therapist, pet sitter, or voice coach. Usually that means building a site that combines content (helpful information for potential clients) and credibility boosters such as articles you have written, testimonials from satisfied clients, and case studies.

An electronic (or email) magazine, called an ezine, is a good credibility-booster. You publish a newsletter for current and potential clients and deliver it via email. The ezine builds a bond with prospects for a tiny fraction of the cost of a paper newsletter. An ezine also lets you capture email addresses of prospects, so you can keep in touch with them and send them special offers.

You might also consider developing an online form that people can use to request more information right on your Web site. Or writing a special report or white paper and turning it into a downloadable document. Visitors must register to receive their copy and in the process you get their email address. In all these cases, the goal of your site is not to make actual sales, but capture qualified leads.

Writing and designing this type of persuasive Web site is beyond the scope of this book. Nevertheless, you will still find a great deal of useful information on the technical nuts-and-bolts behind them in the pages that follow.

Here are some types of businesses that benefit most from persuasive Web sites that establish credibility and capture leads. If you're involved in one of these types of businesses, you may never make actual sales online:

- Professional services such as attorneys, stockbrokers, tax preparers, financial planners, technology consultants, security services, or quality assurance consultants.

- Personal services such as babysitters, day care specialists, house sitters, pet sitters, hair stylists, personal trainers, manicurists, custom tailors, or dry cleaners.

- Therapeutic services such as massage therapists, medical doctors, acupuncturists, osteopaths, dentists, homeopaths, herbalists, or psychologists/counselors.

- Coaching and teaching services such as voice or music teachers, academic tutors, career counselors, dance instructors, business coaching/consulting, or golf teachers.

- Repair or maintenance services such as house cleaners, plumbers, painters, handymen, piano tuners, car mechanics, or wood restorers.

On the other hand, if you are in one of these businesses, you can grow your site into an ecommerce powerhouse later by adding products related to your service. A long-range plan may include creating a unique product and selling it on your Web site. For example, if you are a house sitter, you may be able to write an ebook (electronic book) or special report on home security and safety tips. Whether you sell the product, or give it away to attract clients, you can deliver it online without investing in an inventory of printed books.

Again, don't forget that the nature of Web sites is that they can evolve over time. So as you plot your course, keep some of these options in the back of your mind. But now it's time to talk about something much more personal: Web design.

Web Site Design

Design is a matter of personal taste. That's true whether you are designing printed material, presentations, or Web pages. Nevertheless, the design of your site also says a lot about you and your business. So your design must project the right image.

If your site looks sloppy, thrown together, or out-of-date, so will you! Also, the design goals for an antique store are significantly different from an advertising agency Web site. It is important for the look of your site to accurately represent your industry, as well as your business philosophy.

Before you hire a designer or sit down to build a site yourself, you need to establish the primary design goals for your site. In this section, we help you define your design goals and explain common Web-related issues you should keep in mind because they often determine what is and is not possible when designing a Web page.

At their core, many problems with Web sites have to do with file management. When you surf the 'net and see a "file not found" error, it means the link in the HTML code making up the page is incorrect or the file the link points to is missing. (These are called "broken" links.)

When it comes to Web sites, the word "design" doesn't just mean how the site looks. Plenty of pretty Web sites get no traffic because on the Web, design also incorporates how the site functions. File management is all about organization. When it comes to Web design, your overall design needs to be just as organized as the files that make up the site.

Studies have shown that you get about 10 seconds for people to take in your design and figure out what they want to do. If they can't figure it out, they leave. Your site is just one click away from the rest of the Internet. If you want people to actually stay and visit your site, you need to think about your design.

Avoid designing your Web site as you go along! If you do, you will have to redo a lot of work to accommodate new design concepts. This process can be a nightmare if you have more than a few pages. Even worse, your site will look disjointed. Your navigation will probably confuse visitors. If you confuse visitors, they will leave!

Remember, a clear understanding of what you want to achieve is the most important factor for successful site implementation.

Preliminary Research

One of the best things to do before you even think about the design of your site is to spend some time surfing the Web. Research can make the difference between a design that simply does the job, and one that makes a real impact.

Look for two kinds of sites: those you like and those you don't. Look at sites in your own industry or in related industries. Create two folders in your browser favorites list: Good Sites and Bad Sites. Then add each site as you go along. (Alternatively, you can also simply write down their Web addresses.)

The idea is to record your observations and impressions of these sites. Whether you hire someone else to do your site or create it yourself, the goal is to end up with a site that you enjoy using yourself.

Here are some questions to ask yourself as you study Web sites:

- What catches your eye first? Is it a photo, logo, large headline?

- What makes this site appealing? Blocks of color, overall layout, number of columns, easy-to-read fonts, or something else?

- Why is that site ugly? Is it the colors? Are the fonts too big, or is it something else?

- Why is this site easy to use? Is it because buttons or links are labeled clearly? Do the site sections seem logical?

- Why is that site impossible to figure out? Do you get "lost" in the site? Are there too many pop-ups or flashing graphics that distract you? Is it hard to find your way back or figure out what to do next?

- If you want to buy something, can you find what you're looking for? How many steps does it take? Does the site give you enough information about the product? Are prices easy to find and understand?

- Is the shopping cart easy to use? Are payment procedures easy to understand?

Recording your impressions is worth every moment you spend on this activity. This process will really help you when the time comes to actually design and code your pages. You can communicate the observations to your Web designer, or use them as reference material for yourself as you work on your site.

Always check out your competition. When building a new site, you have a unique opportunity to build something better than the other guy has. Be especially alert to what is missing from your competitors' sites. Missing items can be just as important as what is there. You might even get clues for new products or services, based upon what your competition fails to offer.

As you surf, examine Web sites through the eyes of your customers and prospects. "Taking a walk in your customer's shoes" is the best way to guarantee a good design from the beginning.

Design Goals

Before you start planning your site, figure out what you want to do with it. Remember that the ultimate mission here is always to convince someone to purchase your products or engage your services. If your site doesn't do that, it is not a good use of your business funds.

Figure out the overall point of the site first. Think up a mission statement. Then write it down. Sure, a mission statement sounds like something only big corporate "suits" care about, but think about it: if you don't know what your site is supposed to do, who does?

You don't necessarily have to put this mission statement on the Web site anywhere. In fact, most people don't. But you do have to know what you're doing with your site. Everything in your design has to support that mission. Your specific design goals will come out of your mission statement.

For example, suppose the mission of your site is to sell your handmade soaps. All your goals will be about helping people buy your soaps when they come to your site. Here are some specific goals that would help these people buy:

- Talk about skin problems our customers might have and how our soaps can help.

- Tell them how we make our soaps to build trust in us.

- Show all the ingredients we use, so people see they are getting quality soap.

- Answer any questions they have about how to use our soaps.

- Display photos of all the soaps, so people see exactly what they look like.

- Make it easy for people to find the exact color and scent they want.

- Display exact prices, including shipping costs.

- Show them that their credit card number and personal information is secure.

- Make it easy for them to buy as many different soaps as they want.

- Make it easy for them to pay for their purchase quickly.

- Give them a way to find out when we add new soaps, or when our soaps go on sale.

Do you see how each goal helps people buy your soaps? In fact, these goals are very similar to the goals you would have if you were opening a handmade soap shop in your local mall. It's obvious that when you design your Web site, you'll be designing a shopping experience for your customers.

You want to make sure that everything about your site furthers those shopping goals. Even more importantly, you will want to make triple sure that your site design does not do the opposite of any of those goals!

If your business is therapeutic massage, you probably will not have people paying for massage on your site. (Unless you sell a gift certificate.) Maybe the mission of your site is to get them to contact you for an appointment, or at the very least, request more information about your techniques or prices.

In this case you want to encourage them to feel comfortable contacting you. Here are some specific goals that serve your mission:

- Show people your photo, so they see your smiling, friendly face.

- Show them a photo of someone getting a massage, so they can see the person is modestly draped and very relaxed.

- Talk about how your particular massage skills reduce or eliminate pain for people who suffer from carpal tunnel, fibromyalgia, migraine headache, or sports injuries.

- Tell them about your training in massage, your experience, and your credentials, so they feel you are an expert and know what you're doing.

- Give them some helpful tips for stretches and exercises that will make them feel better in between massages.

- Offer them a free report you have written on how massage helps people quickly recuperate from surgery, illness, or injury.

- Display plenty of testimonials from satisfied clients who really love your massages.

- Show a photo of your massage clinic, with detailed driving and parking instructions, along with a map.

- Explain your prices and the discounts you offer to repeat customers.

- Encourage people to email, call, or even stop by your office, by putting all your contact information on every page.

- Encourage visitors to fill out a form where they can tell you their particular problem with pain or flexibility, and ask you to call them with advice.

To meet these goals, your Web site will have to include specific design elements. For example, it's easy to see that each page will require prominent contact information. You will also need to have a Web form with the programming to make it work. You also definitely don't want to do anything on your site that makes people uncomfortable or makes it hard for them to get in touch with you.

Before you design one pixel of your Web site, write down as many goals as you can. Setting goals ensures you will avoid major design flaws that turn off customers and prospects.

Avoid a Tangled Web

You have control over how you weave your Web site. Job one is to avoid weaving a tangled one! In our experience, the best way to avoid confusion is to plan carefully. A "bubble diagram" is a great planning tool for thinking through a Web site design.

A bubble diagram is exactly what it sounds like. You draw little circles (i.e., bubbles) on a sheet of paper and connect them with lines. Each bubble represents a Web page. Each line represents a hyperlink connecting two pages.

Before you start drawing your bubble diagram, write down and organize all the information you want to include in your site. In the beginning, don't worry about how that information will be organized; just get it down on paper. This information list should include:

- The main concepts you want to cover in your site.

- A title and general description for every page you think you will need.

Because each page should deal with a single subject, you'll be able to use your information list to make sure you don't forget to include important categories of information. If you are having trouble brainstorming ideas, you might want to try our IdeaWeaver writing and creativity software (http://www.IdeaWeaverSoftware.com). It's free to try out for 30 days.

Once you have completed your information list, look it over and consider how various concepts interrelate. Group the items by category. If necessary, group them into subcategories as well. Once you've completed that, you are ready to draw your first bubble diagram.

- Start with a Home bubble. This bubble is the entry point of your site. For example, if your company bakes gourmet pet treats, your Home page would be "Gourmet Pet Treats from Lick Your Chops Pet Bakery."

- Then draw a bubble for each category. Connect these new bubbles to the Home bubble. For example, your main categories might be Dog Treats, Cat Treats, Parrot Treats, Lizard Treats, Treat Ingredients, Pet Feeding Tips, and Using Treats As Rewards.

- If you have subcategories, draw them in their own bubble. Then connect them to the appropriate category. For example, you might have Large Dog Treats, Small Dog Treats, Puppy Treats, Cat Treats, Kitten Treats, Small Parrot Treats, and Cockatiel Treats.

- Finally, draw your page bubbles and connect them to their category or subcategory bubble. For example, you'll want a Contact page (so people know how to get in touch with you), an Order page, and maybe a Pet Treat FAQ (Frequently Asked Questions) page.

Your bubble diagram is a graphical representation of your site. It is like a map. It shows you how visitors will navigate to find the information they seek. The lines represent links, and show you how many times your visitor will have to click to find what they want. This step is important; you do not want to make it hard for your visitor to figure out what to do!

You can use a bubble diagram for a high-level overview or to make a detailed map of one particular section of your site.

Understanding Your Bubble Diagram

Okay, now that you've drawn your bubble diagram, study it. First, notice how your bubble diagram shows that you need to plan ahead for transitional material in your Web site. By transitional material, we mean the information in your site that helps connect your pages logically, so they build on each other.

Your Home page should introduce your entire site. In the Lick Your Chops example, it tells people up front that Lick Your Chops makes all-natural, gourmet pet treats, and that they can buy those treats right here on your Web site. (Whatever you do, don't make your visitors guess what your site is about!)

Your Home page is your most general page. From now on, every link from your Home page must go someplace logical. It would make sense for your Category and Subcategory pages to deal with different aspects of what you sell.

The Subcategories will build on the general information on the Category pages. The information on your Category pages will introduce and summarize the details that appear in your Subcategory pages.

For example, when your visitors click on Products, they should not go to Kitten Treats. They should go to a Category page that gives general information about all the different treats you make. There, they might find links to other Subcategory pages, like Large Dog Treats, and Small Dog Treats.

Can you see how this kind of logical architecture helps your visitors? They can easily make sense of your site organization. When you create a site where visitors can find things easily, you help them to buy. Obviously buying is good for your business!

Second, your bubble diagram helps you decide what your site's navigational menu should look like. Each Category should be a menu item, and Subcategories should appear as links on the Category page or on a menu that drops down from the Category menu item.

Use your bubble diagram to test your site organization. Pretend that you are looking for a specific piece of information on one of your pages. If you start at the Home page, does the organization you chose naturally lead you to the information you want? Follow the lines on your diagram, remembering that each of those lines is a click. Here's a sample bubble diagram for our IdeaWeaver site (http://www. IdeaWeaverSoftware.com).

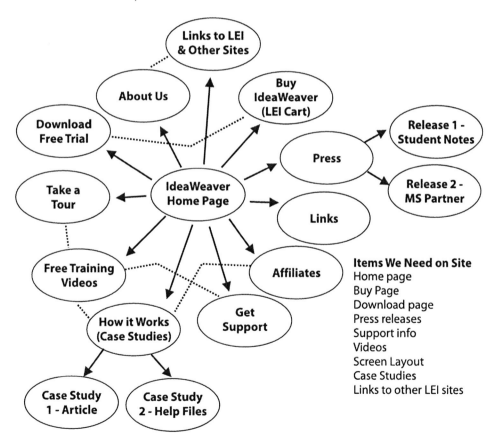

Most experts suggest that pages be no more than two clicks from the Home page, so try to keep your hierarchy as simple as possible. If people can't figure out your site, they will leave your site.

After you're happy with the diagram, ask a friend who was not involved in the organizing process to try the same test a few times. Can they easily see the flow from one bubble to another?

The art of proper Web site organization lies in how easy it is to retrieve what you want. It's much easier to fix navigation problems on paper than it is to recode links on many pages!

Now for the hard part: If your diagram doesn't cut it, don't be reluctant to start over. Don't become attached to the diagram. It's just a tool. The goal here is to create a Web site, not a bubble diagram. Plus, if you know your Web site may evolve and grow over time, take that into account. Think of it as a tree with branches. Consider where it makes sense to grow a new "branch" so you have the flexibility to add pages later without having to tear apart the entire site.

Remember that every time you scrunch up the paper and start over, you just saved yourself hundreds or even thousands of dollars in Web development fees! Your bubble diagram helps you do it right, so you won't have to do it over.

Finding a Web Developer

Once you have a plan for your site, it's time to make a big decision. Whether you're creating your first Web site or significantly updating an existing site, you have probably considered hiring a professional Web developer to do the work for you.

However, hiring an experienced designer/developer is not a low-cost proposition!

To save money, you may be considering doing the work yourself or having one of your employees do it for you. If so, remember that producing a good Web site requires specialized tools and techniques and an aptitude for learning both. When you hire a professional, you are paying for that aptitude.

Owning a copy of FrontPage doth not a good designer make. The Web is littered with proof. If you don't have design and development aptitude in-house, please don't risk your company's professional image on an amateur Web site. Remember all those ugly sites you saw when you were doing preliminary research? You don't want your site to be one of them!

When looking for a professional, you'll need to evaluate his or her qualifications. It's difficult to evaluate someone's skills if you don't know much about the subject yourself. So your first and most important step should be to figure out how you want your Web site to work. This knowledge will guide and protect you.

If you have a clear, detailed idea of the functionality of your site, you'll be less likely to get distracted by the merely attractive, but not functional, elements of your site.

If you haven't done your research and created a good bubble diagram yet, stop now! Go back to the beginning of this section and do your research. Examine other Web sites. Note the features you see that you would like to incorporate into your own site. Draw several bubble diagrams until you have a navigation plan that flows logically.

All these notes and pictures will give you a common reference point and will show a potential developer that you know what you want. Most Web site development firms give you a free initial consultation to discuss your site. You should always bring notes and diagrams to these meetings.

As for where exactly to look for a Web developer, you can check online freelance sites like Guru or Elance. Or take the old-fashioned approach and look in the phone book under Web Site Design.

Essential Questions to Ask Before You Hire

Whether you find a developer online or locally, you should ask a few important questions.

1. What services do they offer?

The more complex your ecommerce site, the more important this question becomes. You can frequently save money, time, and aggravation if you have a single point of contact for all Web site issues.

If the firm offers all the design, programming, ecommerce, and hosting solutions you need, this can be a huge plus! Consider taking advantage of any package deal they offer. Or simply ask them to cut you a deal for bundled services.

2. Is it easy to communicate with this firm?

You need to feel comfortable working with the people who will be doing your site design and development. Successful communication is critical to a successful project. If they don't seem to understand what you want, or they don't make you feel confident that they can do the job, talk to another firm before making a decision.

Always beware of designers and developers who…

- Don't listen. If they talk more than you do, be careful!

- Are condescending and seem unable or unwilling to explain things to you without resorting to a lot of jargon.

- Have no real-life business experience.

- Seem more interested in how your site looks than how it functions. Or vice versa.

Remember, you are the customer. You know your business. You are building your Web site to increase sales, not to add to the portfolio or resume of your Web developer and designer.

3. Do you like the sites they have created in the past?

Graphic design is very subjective and personal. If you don't like the work the designers produced for others, you probably won't like what they produce for you.

4. Will any of the work be subcontracted?

Most firms don't call attention to the fact that they use subcontractors. Until something goes wrong, that is! Then you hear excuses about how the subcontractor failed to perform. Make sure the firm you hire takes ultimate responsibility for completing your project, regardless of how it is accomplished.

5. Is the firm willing to give references?

If a Web design/development firm isn't comfortable giving references, move on. You'll be making a substantial investment in your Web site. Like any employer, you have a right to talk to some references. You don't have to go overboard; one or two satisfied customers are enough. If possible, ask the firm for references from people who are in your line of business.

If you are hiring someone over the Internet through a site like Guru.com, you may be inundated with responses to your project posting. Even though we DO Web design, we have outsourced various projects when we felt we were just too close to the problem or completely overwhelmed with work. Here are a few hints for hiring over the Internet, based on our experience.

a. Be very, very specific in your requirements.

Explain what you do and also what you do *not* want. Here is an example of one of our project postings to give you an idea. (Don't worry about all the acronyms now; you'll know them by the end of this book!)

```
We need someone with experience in creating Web sites that load
quickly and use plain text navigation and minimal graphics.

You need to understand the following:

HMTL coding - You have to be able to READ and understand HTML
without using a WYSIWYG tool. If you use a Macintosh, Adobe
GoLive or FrontPage, please do not apply. (Dreamweaver is okay,
but you need to actually look at code view and understand what
you're seeing!)

Cascading Style Sheets - Again, you have to understand how CSS
works, not just how a software product works.

Photoshop and optimizing Web graphics. If you have decided that
"everyone has Flash" please don't apply.

The bottom line is that you absolutely have to understand HTML
and CSS and have created extremely optimized fast-loading sites
in the past.

The other requirement is that you must be a full-time freelancer
who uses a PC. Sorry Mac users, but please do not apply. (And
don't ask...I'm not changing my mind.)
```

b. To whittle down the responses, include questions in the posting that are based on your requirements.

Anyone who doesn't answer the questions can be immediately ditched because clearly they can't follow instructions. (You wouldn't believe how many people just provide a canned response without answering the questions!)

Here's another example from the same posting.

Please answer the following questions to be considered. Canned responses without answers to the questions will be forwarded to the big data dumpster in the sky.

Questions:

1. Do you use a PC?

2. What software do you use?

3. Have you created sites using CSS?

4. Do you have a portfolio with links to live sites you've created?

5. Are you a full-time freelancer and what is your attitude toward deadlines?

Because you've planned out your site and know what you want, finding a Web developer you can work with actually should not be very difficult. Out of 50 or 60 responses, we usually end up with about 10 or fewer people who actually answer the questions intelligently and meet our criteria.

We look at the portfolios and see if we like their designs. That weeds out a few more. Finally, we post a message to the best contenders and ask about their availability. If someone seems good, we ask to set up a time to talk to them on the phone.

Remember, getting a custom-designed Web site can be a fairly expensive proposition. So it's worth it to take the time to find a designer you can work with.

Don't Buy Into the Hype

You may have noticed in the last section that our job posting actually specifically said no Mac or FrontPage people should apply. The reasons for that have nothing to do with whether or not we think Macintoshes have a superior or inferior operating system. We have no interest in getting into some Mac-PC debate with our contractor. The reason is more mundane: file compatibility. We use a PC and Dreamweaver, so it's just simpler to work with contractors who do too.

Along the same lines, every once in a while, one of our potential clients will ask us what we recommend for a hosting environment (Windows, UNIX, or Linux), site development tool (Dreamweaver, GoLive), or database system (MySQL, SQL Server). Questions on specific technologies raise a little warning flag with us. Why? They are usually a veiled invitation to a religious discussion on the merits of the questioner's pet environment!

As someone who is hiring a Web development firm, don't fall into the trap of thinking one type of technology is somehow superior to another. If the Web developer makes a big deal about how they use a Mac because it's superior, or host on Windows servers because they are "better," be suspicious. Focus on what the technology can do, not on what someone is parroting from some technology magazine.

Be especially wary of the hype that comes from "technology consultants." These people are often enamored of the theory behind the technology. They like to push the latest and greatest. They aren't always up to speed on whether the technology is reliable, easy to maintain, and cost-effective in real world environments.

We have a saying at our company: "It's just another operating system."

In fact, you can replace the words operating system with programming language, database system, or any other class of technology.

We have worked with far too many different environments to fall prey to the bigotry that polarizes a lot of the Web development community. Do we think we are somehow enlightened? No.

Technology is just a tool. It's a means to an end. For you, the end is to produce a Web site that helps customers buy from you quickly, easily, and accurately. Your customers won't know, or care, whether that happens on a Windows or Linux machine.

Don't Pay for More Than You Have To

When choosing a Web design/development firm, you will sometimes run into firms that try to talk you into spending more money than necessary. These firms often have many high-powered customers with big budgets.

Say you ask this type of firm for a clean, simple, straightforward ecommerce site. They respond by showing off several big, complicated, glitzy sites they've done for other clients, bragging about the large number of sales that are generated by these sites. Don't be taken in!

Instead, view these "super-sites" with a critical eye. Is the site really easy to use? How long does it take to load the site on a home PC with a slow connection? Could the site do the same things using a simpler interface?

We have worked with too many clients who have wasted a lot of money on sites that are hard to use. They fell for a sales pitch given by Web developers who are guilty of spreading hype about their favorite tools. These developers aren't necessarily dishonest. They're just so crazy about technology, they lose sight of your primary business objective.

Here is what can happen if you fall for the techno-hype from a less than honest firm. The salespeople may claim that your site may not need extra bells and whistles now. But the sales pitch will imply that you will soon want them, since more and more people "expect" them. Then they will talk you into extra graphics or scripts that you probably really don't need.

As with many high-pressure sales pitches, what they don't say is more important than what they do say. For example, the high-pressure sales folks won't tell you that:

- Your visitors may leave your site before it finishes downloading because it's too big and takes too long to appear in their browser.

- The next release of Internet Explorer or another browser may break your site. Of course, Microsoft and AOL will say they have "enhanced" the browser. In the meantime, your scripts have stopped working.

- Your visitors may think the Flash animation is cool the first time, but they find it annoying from then on and skip it.

You will discover these "omissions" later. (Usually when you have to pay this unscrupulous firm to fix it or undo all these "cool" extras!)

Stay away from any Web development firm that tries to convince you that you just can't live without that Flash animation, graphical menu with rollovers, or JavaScript-intensive feature. Otherwise you'll end up with "features" you not only don't need, but that mess up your visitor's shopping experience and possibly the ability for anyone to find the site in the first place.

Our bottom line advice is simple: stay away from anything glitzy, especially for your first site. Keep your requirements focused on the business reasons you have for creating your Web site in the first place.

How to Protect Yourself

To protect yourself from falling for a slick sales pitch, always think about what is best for the people visiting your site. Someone who wants to buy your car alarms, ebooks, or dog treats could really care less about whether you use the latest Web design tools with the fanciest features.

Customers have simple goals. They want to:

- Find products or information fast.

- Get information that will help them make a purchase decision.

- Buy without hassle.

Your customers' goals should really be your goals, too! It's your developer's job to make sure your Web site achieves these goals. If your Web site design fails to accomplish your prime directive of meeting your customers' goals, it won't matter how powerful or state-of-the-art the underlying technology is.

Sometimes Web sites do fail. Miserably. On the "bleeding edge" of technology the blood is usually the customer's! In other words: yours. Remember you are going to be the one footing the bill for a site that doesn't result in sales.

New technologies take time to master, and customers expect to have their applications built by a master, not a novice. Be careful of Web developers/designers who are pushing the "hottest" technologies. Make sure they have built a few complete projects that use the new technology. Make sure those sites work and the clients are happy with them. The bottom line is that you don't want a developer learning his new pet technology on your Web site with you footing the bill.

What does this lecture on new technology have to do with doing business on the Web? It comes back to the point that you shouldn't worry about underlying technology. That subject should be very low on your list of concerns. Your focus should be on usability and reliability, in that order.

Why usability first? Because if customers love your site, they will come back even if they find it's unavailable once in a blue moon. Think about simple sites like CraigsList. com. It has nothing but text, but it's well organized, fast, and extremely usable, so it's become incredibly popular.

If your visitors found your site to be a time and energy waster the first time they visit, they won't come back! If customers can't use your site the first time around, you've lost them forever.

Remember, all technology is basically "dead end technology." Anything related to computers has a terribly short life span, so let your business requirements dictate when it makes sense to rebuild and take advantage of the latest and greatest tools.

Remember, the latest is not necessarily the greatest. Be prepared to tone down the enthusiasm of your Web developer. Get off on the right foot by looking for developers and designers who place a priority on producing the best Web shopping experience for you and your customers.

Web Site Content

Building a Web site is not rocket science. You must approach your site logically, so you don't get carried away or intimidated by the technological aspects.

Although it might not seem like it at first glance, your site's navigation is easily one of the most important aspects of your site's content. Always make it easy for your visitors to navigate your site with clear, logical site navigation. By site navigation, we are talking about the links your visitors use to move from one page to another. Your approach to navigation can actually make or break your site because it has a significant affect on your site's performance and usability.

Earlier, we talked about the benefits of using a bubble diagram to organize your site. You'll find that when designing your site navigation this diagram will be invaluable. Organization is key. Although it is possible to give visitors direct access to virtually every page of the site (a site map page frequently does just that), visitors will feel more comfortable if their browsing experience is guided by an intelligent and logical organization of your material.

Set Up Smart Site Navigation

If visitors can progress through your site logically, they will never have trouble finding what they need. Combine good navigation with transition pages that introduce a group of related information pages, and visitors will never get lost.

A navigation menu is a set of links that appear on every page. Your visitors will use this menu for quick access to the most important features of your site. Building a navigation menu for a well-organized site is much easier than building one for a poorly organized site!

Your navigation menu should give visitors immediate access to all of the major transition pages in your site. From these transition pages, visitors get closer to what they are looking for. If they have clicked the wrong link, they can quickly realize what they need to click in order to get back on track.

You can construct your navigation menu in a variety of ways. However, most navigation solutions are a combination of two possibilities: graphical versus non-graphical, and scripted versus non-scripted.

Graphical refers to whether or not you use graphic images for your navigation links. Scripted refers to whether or not you use JavaScript to create special effects in reaction to mouse movement.

We have a bias for non-graphical, non-scripted navigation because it generally works on all browsers and it's efficient. Using graphics for navigation can make your site quite attractive. It also means the browser must download those graphics, which slows down your site. You will need to hire a graphic designer to create the images and to make new ones if you add more pages or change the wording in the future. So graphical navigation always adds an additional expense to the site-building budget.

The biggest reason not to use JavaScript for navigation is that many times it can't be read by search engines, so the spiders can't access the pages on your site. Java also can generate browser errors. Error messages annoy visitors, sometimes causing them to leave your site altogether. Depending on the complexity of the desired effects and the tools being used, JavaScript may also add to the design costs of your site.

Do you have your heart set on using buttons, navigation bars with rollovers, and other "jazzy" navigation effects? It is perfectly feasible to use both graphics and scripting safely if you know what you are doing.

If you go this route, you must be willing to test your work on every browser you intend to support. If you don't, you risk losing traffic and sales if your pages load too slowly or don't render well in older browsers.

No matter what method you use, your main navigation menu should give your visitors an easy way to reach all of the major areas of your site. If your site is fairly large, you may want to introduce an additional menu on your transition pages that is positioned under, or next to, the main menu.

This new menu gives your visitors access to more specific transition pages. It should appear on every page under the major area. Using your transition pages and this cascading menu approach makes it easy for visitors to drill down through your site and find exactly what they are looking for, even if your site has hundreds of pages.

If you feel comfortable adding scripting into your site, you can build the cascading menu effect right into the main navigation menu. When visitors position their mouse over a menu item, the related sub-menu drops down or flies out from it.

This feature can provide a quick way to get to virtually any page of the site from any other page. It has also been criticized as "mystery meat" navigation because you don't know the feature exists unless you happen to position your mouse over the menu long enough to trigger the drop-down.

Once your site is built, you may want to take a close look at your site statistics and provide a Most Popular Pages menu item. This link takes visitors to a transition page with direct links to the pages that are most often accessed. Another possibility is the Most Recent Pages menu item. This menu option sends visitors to a list of the most recently added or changed information pages. Naturally, you want to include these information pages in your normal navigation scheme as well.

As you build your site, always keep one eye on your organization and navigation structure. After your site is finished, periodically review your navigation and ask yourself if it can be improved. Enhancing the usability of your site navigation can substantially enhance your visitor's experience, even if you don't change one word of the content!

Lay the Groundwork

The Home page is the first thing to consider. It must clearly and succinctly explain what your site is about and why anyone should care. We've all seen sites that are completely mystifying; don't make yours one of them. Next, use clear, obvious navigation so that people can get where they want to go quickly. On a large site, that means you should group related information together. Don't make people guess which link might take them to the information they want. People don't want to guess and they'll just leave instead.

If you are still having trouble figuring out how to organize your site, spend some time looking at other sites. If every other site in your industry has a link called Contact that links to a page with the corporate phone numbers, follow the trend and name your navigational elements similarly. Again, people are at your site to get information; don't make them hunt for it.

Remember that creating a Web site is really a lot like creating a physical storefront. You have certain business requirements. The most important is making sales! Logic dictates that people won't make a purchase unless they feel comfortable about parting with their money.

Always lay some groundwork to convince your visitors that you are for real. You can convince them in a number of ways. Here are a few of the best ways to make people feel that they have come to the right place to spend money!

Identify Your Company

The first thing visitors want to know is who you are and what you do. Your Home page should clearly identify your business and describe the major products or services you offer. At the very least, your Home page should function as a business card or brochure.

Be concise on your Home page. Get to the point. You only have a few moments to grab the attention of your visitors and convince them to stay.

Explain Your Competitive Advantage

The next thing your visitors want to know is why they should buy from you instead of your competition. Your Home page should include the reasons why your customers buy from you and why they come back to buy again later.

After you identify yourself and your business, describe the advantages you offer that win customers and keep them coming back. Don't just *say* you are the best. Visitors want to know *why* you are the best. How can they possibly know unless you tell them?

Compel Visitors to Buy

Remember that the most important information on your site invites visitors to place an order. Whether people order on your Web site or over the phone, they must understand how to order. So starting with the Home page, you should shepherd new visitors through your site to the order point.

Don't make visitors search for a way to buy from you. Your site should present the opportunity to order right up front, and the rest of the site should reinforce the desire to buy from you.

People like to buy from someone they know, so tell them about yourself from the beginning. Communicate your expertise. Share your knowledge and credentials, and don't be afraid to let your personality come through.

People buy from people, not machines. When you tell your visitor about your personal and professional background, they get to know you better. In their eyes, you become a personable and competent guide, not just a salesperson. So when you lead them to the sales point, they are more comfortable making a purchase.

If you are having trouble getting your ideas together, check out our IdeaWeaver writing and creativity software (http://www.IdeaWeaverSoftware.com. Even if you won't be the person writing the final copy, any writer you hire will appreciate receiving your notes and thoughts about the content you would like on your site. After all, no one knows your business better than you do!

Present a Consistent Look

What color do you think of when I say, "Target?" I'd be surprised if you said anything other than bright red. Color plays a powerful role in marketing and sales. Colors and logos are an important part of brand identity.

You probably already use certain colors in your logo and printed materials. Your Web site should continue your color theme and build on it. You will find that customers associate these colors with your business, whether you intend them to or not. These colors tie your site to your other marketing materials, creating a polished, professional image.

For similar reasons, use a consistent layout for your Web pages. Visitors tend to learn the layout of your site very quickly. If you put the navigation menu at the top on one page, they will expect it to be there on all the other pages as well.

Consistency in layout helps visitors navigate your site efficiently. It lets them focus on the content that differentiates each page of your site, instead of hunting for buttons and links.

Perhaps the most important aspect of Web site design can be stated in two words: minimize confusion!

Remember that your visitors can leave your site in one click. Why give them reason to do so? They are shopping online to save time, not waste it! If you make your site difficult to navigate, people will simply go to your competitors.

If your site is confusing, your credibility suffers. With so many clear, easy-to-use Web sites out there, visitors expect a certain usability standard. If your site doesn't deliver this clarity, your business as well as your Web site appears amateurish.

Use your corporate logo and colors on your site. Use a consistent framework for your site pages. Put your logo and navigation elements in the same location on every page. If you follow these simple rules, your visitors won't be distracted. They will focus on the content of your site and buy from you.

Provide Answers

Remember that at its heart, the Internet is about information. The goal of any site is to provide information to visitors. To establish credibility with your visitors, it helps to anticipate their questions and provide an easy way to get answers. By explaining the important concepts related to your industry, you demonstrate your expertise. You also help your customer make an informed buying decision. Customers appreciate this effort because they trust someone who has their best interests at heart.

One of the most useful aspects of a Web site is the fact that it is a hypertext medium. Hypertext refers to the way you can link content from one page to related content on another page. The power of this feature is that you can put a lot of information on your site without overwhelming visitors with it all at once. People can drill down into the topics that interest them, and skip over those topics that don't.

One way to present answers is to literally create a Frequently Asked Questions (FAQ) page. This technique is effective because it allows you to anticipate customer objections. You can tackle potential concerns up front and increase your odds of closing sales. Plus you can also save yourself many individual email queries from potential customers, and experience fewer customer support phone calls.

A Frequently Asked Questions page works best with a limited number of questions. Once you have more than about ten, it becomes cumbersome for your visitors to scan them. They need to do too much hunting to find the question they are interested in!

An alternative is to present the answers in an information section organized topically. This approach has an advantage over an FAQ page in that you can present the answers alongside other concepts that help explain the why of it all.

What material is appropriate for an FAQ page or an information section? Just think back on the questions your customers ask your salespeople and what they call you about. If your current customers need that information, so do your Web site visitors.

Keep It Simple

When it comes to your Web site, you want to avoid confusion at all costs. Nothing will drive a customer away faster than a confusing site.

Planning your site organization in advance is critical to building a coherent visitor experience. Visitors expect good navigation, and won't tolerate confusion. So create as many bubble diagrams as necessary so you can get the organization right before you start designing pages.

Finally, you obviously want to make your site visually appealing, but use graphics judiciously (we'll discuss this more in the next section). Irrelevant images are distracting; use meaningful images that enhance your message. Also never, ever sacrifice readability to accommodate some Web designer's warped sense of cool. Far, far too many people have ended up with unusable sites that they hate because they were afraid to say "no" to their Web designer. Yes, design is subjective, but you're a Web citizen too and if you hate using your Web site, I promise you, other people will too. Visitors don't return to a business site because of the pretty pictures. They return for the content.

You should be aware of these tips even if you aren't the one designing your site. You are the one who knows your business. Your Web designer needs your guidance in order to produce a site that will work well for you. If you insist on these key elements when working with a designer, you can avoid a needless and expensive site redesign down the road.

Web Site Graphics

Graphics are the easiest way to introduce unique design elements into your site. But that benefit can come at a cost to download time. Every graphic, no matter how small, increases the time it takes for your pages to load in a browser. Have you ever stared at a blank page, waiting for something to appear… and then hit the Back button in frustration? You aren't the only one. Every visitor who does that at your site is a potential lost sale.

Keep in mind that many of your site visitors may be using a dial-up connection of 56K or less. If your site is overloaded with graphic content, you will drive those visitors away. As we said earlier, there's a reason why somewhat graphically "plain" sites like CraigsList and Yahoo are popular.

Use Web Graphic Formats

Because download speed is so important, your images should be as small as possible. By small, we don't just mean the height and width of your image. Three factors affect the size of your image files:

- Dimensions: The width and height of the image, in pixels.

- Color Depth: The number of different colors used.

- Compression: What form of compression the image uses, if any.

In general, you want to create an image that has exactly the dimensions you need, no more colors than necessary, and uses as much compression as possible without making the image look bad.

GIF and JPEG Formats

The two most common graphics formats on the Web are GIF (Graphics Interchange Format) and JPEG (Joint Photographic Experts Group). Each format has characteristics that make it useful for specific applications.

Neither format is intrinsically better than the other. Deciding which format to use depends on the type of image and what you'll be doing with it. Both GIF and JPEG are compressed bitmap image formats, which is why they are popular for Web use. Small file size equals faster download time.

GIF uses lossless compression, which removes redundant information from the image without sacrificing quality. JPEG uses lossy compression, which removes redundant information and reduces similar colors to a single average color (this process is known as interpolation).

With a JPEG image, you will lose some of the original information in the image. However, you also can control how much interpolation is performed. You can select the compression level for your JPEG image. More compression lowers the quality, so you can select a compression level that produces the smallest file that still has an acceptable display quality.

In general, you want to use a GIF file for images that must render exactly as created and that consist of blocks of color. Most company logos and clip art fit these characteristics. These files typically utilize a limited color palette.

JPEG files are usually used for continuous-tone images like photographs. As you increase the compression level of a JPEG, the compression produces artifacts. These artifacts make the image look grainy or distorted.

The more you compress, the smaller the image becomes—and the more noticeable the artifacts become. Fortunately, your eye is much less likely to notice the artifacts introduced by JPEG's lossy compression scheme in a photo, where colors, tones, and shadow blend together and hide the artifacts.

Because many Web visitors still use a 56K modem (or slower) to reach your site, every byte counts. Most design guides recommend a total page size of 40KB or less. As you can see, when it comes to graphics, size really does matter!

Whether you choose GIF or JPEG format for your image, your goal is the same: to produce the smallest image possible that still looks acceptable on your Web page. This technique is called optimizing your images. Here are some tips for achieving good-looking, optimized images:

- Use GIF for logos, clip art, and other images with blocks of color.

- Use the JPEG format for photographs and other images that include a color gradient or screen.

- Create the image at the size you need. Don't create an image that is 600 by 400 and then display it in a 300 by 200 box. The browser still has to download the entire image.

- Reduce your color palette to use just the colors required by the image. Using a true-color palette for two-color line art is pointless.

- If you are not very comfortable making color choices, limit your options by just using colors from the Web-safe palette. Only 216 colors render the same way across the common Web platforms. Most image editing programs provide this palette for you to use with your Web images.

- Avoid using graphics for text or navigation. Careful use of color and fonts makes it unnecessary to replace text with images that contain nothing but text. We've seen dozens of sites that have graphics made up of Arial text on a solid background. There's NO reason to ever do this because you can achieve exactly the same look without using a graphic.

- Within reason, merge adjacent or related images into one larger image wherever possible. Every image requires a separate connection to the Web server, which introduces extra overhead. It is faster to download one 4KB image than four 1KB images.

- Use alternate text to avoid "blank box" syndrome. Alternate text puts labels in your images so visitors can see what is going on before the page finishes loading.

Alternate text is also important for visually impaired visitors. These people often use accessibility tools called "screen readers" to surf the Internet. The screen reader literally reads the page out loud and will read the alternate text to describe the graphics for the visitor. Meaningful descriptions in your alternate text can help these people use your Web site.

More on Alt Text

Earlier we said: when it comes to your site, you want to avoid confusion. It's also important to avoid frustration.

For example, here's a frustrating browsing experience: you click on a page that is mostly graphics, then wait forever with no clue what those graphics are for. Until your browser downloads the images, all you see is a bunch of empty blocks.

We also mentioned alternate (or alt) text. If you use alt text, those blocks won't be empty (unless the visitor has specifically configured his browser not to display alt text). Many Web development tools do not have any automatic way to help you add alt text. But it's worth it to go back into the code and set this attribute in the HTML, so you don't end up with a page of empty image blocks.

If you include alt text, the text shows until the browser replaces the block with the downloaded image. In some browsers, this text also appears when you hover your mouse over the image.

Alternate text helps your visitors navigate your site more quickly. It can also be used to provide a text interpretation of the buttons and icons you use. If the graphic is a link and you can see where it will go by reading the alternate text, you can usually click on the graphic immediately and move on to the next page without having to wait for the first one to finish downloading.

And as we noted before, alternate text is also important for accessibility reasons. Visitors using screen readers need alt text. You may think that it's not a big deal for your site, but do you really want to shut out your site to ANY users?

Avoid Using Graphics for Navigation or Text

This recommendation will come as a big disappointment to a lot of you. Many people are enamored of the slick look produced by graphic pull-down menus and rollover link graphics. However, as mentioned earlier, graphic intensity comes at a high price to performance.

Why avoid rollover images on your site? Because each rollover requires two graphics: the on graphic and the off graphic. Having two graphics increases the time your page takes to load. Is this effect really worth it, when it tries the patience of your visitors?

Using graphics to depict only text is a waste of bandwidth. Why waste this precious bandwidth on words, especially when you might need it for more important things, like pictures of your products? Most of the time, careful use of fonts and colors can achieve the look you want without resorting to yet another image.

Another reason to use real text for the text on your page is because text is what the search engines read. We talk a lot more about search engines later in the book, but briefly, navigation menus are often made up of keywords that are relevant to your site. For example, if you sell pet products, you might have Collars and Leashes as a category in your shopping cart.

When a search engine is scanning (or indexing) your site, it is looking for relevant keywords to figure out what your site is about. Search engines can't read graphics; they read text. If the menus are text, they almost always help the search engines do their job, which is to bring visitors to your site that are interested in what you are offering.

Limit Image Size and Quantity

Optimizing your image files is important, but still only part of the total picture. You must also be careful how you use images on your Web pages.

We already explained that you want to keep your Web pages down to about 40KB in total size so your page doesn't take ages to download on a slow connection. That 40KB includes all HTML code and the graphics. Anything more than that produces a sluggish Web site that is frustrating to navigate, especially on dial-up.

The number of images on your page is almost as important as the size of those images. As we pointed out, every image requires a separate connection to the Web server. Knowing this situation, you can make certain decisions that will speed up your site. For example, perhaps you accept Visa, MasterCard, American Express, and Discover for online payment, and you want to put those logos on your site. It is better to create a single image with all four logos together than it is to use four separate images.

If you have a broadband connection to the Internet, remember that what you see is at least five times faster than what dial-up visitors see. The only way to be sure how your site performs is to access it through a modem connection. If you think people will happily wait for your overloaded pages to download, think again!

You can only get away with long downloads on pages specifically designated for multiple photographs or large amounts of text. Visitors are more likely to put up with the wait if they expect to get a page full of images. People on dial-up will often patiently wait for photos to download because they understand that pages full of graphics take time to render. If they've decided they need to see photos to help them make a purchase decision, they don't mind the wait.

However, what does annoy visitors is *unnecessarily* long downloads. Never put pages full of graphics in your critical navigation path! Also make sure you warn visitors about any links that can take a while to download, such as large PDFs, video or audio files. If you have links to a separate file, *always* say what type of file it is and how large it is, so visitors can decide whether or not they want to click the link.

Unfortunately, this lack of courtesy is becoming more common online. People using dial-up connections will just close the window and leave your site forever if they accidentally click an unmarked link to a 5MB PDF file.

One way to give visitors access to a large number of photographs is to offer a thumbnail page. A thumbnail page shows scaled-down versions of your images. When visitors click on a particular thumbnail image, you display the full-sized photo on another page.

This approach gives your visitors the best of both worlds. They don't have to wait a long time to get a quick look at your products because thumbnails are small. They also get to choose which images they need to see up close. When you give visitors more control over which long download times are most important to them, you have happier visitors!

Scripting, Plug-ins, Animations, and Sound

As the Internet becomes more popular, more and more software applications are moving onto Web servers. People using these applications are basically running software through a browser-based user interface. You don't have the software installed on your computer. The software is installed on a server someplace, and you make it do things through your browser.

To offer users an experience that rivaled PC software, vendors needed to give developers a way to extend the browser interface. They started to develop tools to make browsers do things they were not originally designed to do. JavaScript is one of the most popular tools for client-side (browser) scripting. Now you may hear references to Ajax as well, but really it's just another form of JavaScript. (Technically, it stands for Asynchronous JavaScript and XML.)

Unfortunately, every vendor implements the JavaScript language differently and defines the rules for manipulating the browser differently! This situation makes it extremely difficult to develop a rich user experience that works across all browsers.

What does this mean for your ecommerce Web site? You should be very careful about adding features to your site that rely exclusively on JavaScript. In particular, you should never use a script-based menu system as the only way for visitors to navigate your site. Always, always include a text-based alternative as well.

If you're trying to decide whether using JavaScript is worth the potential pitfalls, ask yourself these questions:

- Can you remember a time when you got some kind of scripting error while navigating to a Web page?

- After you got the error, where you able to navigate through the site anyway? Or were you stuck?

- How did you feel about that site after you got the error?

- Would you want your visitors to have that feeling about your site?

The fact is a lot of scripting is totally unnecessary. Usually you can use simpler, less tricky methods to achieve the same results. Also, some browsers simply don't support Java, and some people intentionally turn it off. If you do use scripting, use it sparingly and be sure to test it on all the browsers you care to support.

Plug-ins are just as bad. A plug-in is a separate piece of software that your user must download before they can experience sound, movies, and other bells and whistles on your site. Some people don't want to take the extra time, and bandwidth, to download extra software. They may not have space on their hard drive for the plug-in. Or they find the whole idea just plain scary!

Flash is an example of a common plug-in. To view Flash animation, you must download a sizable program. Realistically, Flash animations are cool the first time, boring the second time, and annoying beyond that. Plus, not too long ago, Internet Explorer updated itself, so everyone had to re-download the Flash plug-in to avoid getting an error message.

With this in mind, it should come as no surprise that we recommend never using a Flash animation as the only way for people to enter your site. It is like locking the front door of your business and requiring customers to get a key from somewhere down the street!

Use animations when they make sense as part of your content. They can be extremely helpful, for example, when demonstrating how to assemble something, or to show exactly how something looks when it moves. Visitors appreciate this type of useful animation, so they won't mind waiting for it to load.

Just use the same precautions with useful animations as you would with any other bandwidth-intensive file. Make sure you warn your visitors that they will have to wait for the animation to load. Never put these pages in your critical navigation path.

Remember that frivolous animations of any kind are annoying to most people. If you are trying to read the content of a page, the last thing you want is a distracting graphic flashing in the periphery. In fact, flashing can cause seizures in some people, which is not exactly the type of visitor experience you're after.

If you're using the animation just because it's "cool," it detracts from the businesslike and professional image you want to project. Gratuitous animation can make you look amateurish and destroy your credibility.

Use sound as you would use an animation: only when it supports the content. For example, if you sell duck calls, you could include a sample of what each one sounds like. That sample should only play when the customer clicks a link requesting it though. Never force people to listen to music when the site opens. This awful use of sound is probably one of our biggest pet peeves, and we're not alone!

Web Site Extras

Once you have a basic site up, you can add many things to it. As we pointed out, most sites evolve over time. Our business Web site (http://www.logicalexpressions.com) has more than 200 pages now. But it didn't start out that way. In this section, we give you an overview of some of the additional "goodies" you might want to add to your site.

Online Forms

Online, it's common to offer visitors the opportunity to fill out a form and submit it via email to someone at your organization. Examples include: a request for additional information, a questionnaire, or a feedback form. Including a simple contact form, instead of a link to your email address also keeps your email address hidden, so spammers are less likely to pick it up.

Creating the form itself is a fairly simple exercise with HTML or a visual Web page editor. Sending the form contents via email requires program support on the server. If you ask, most hosting companies will give you the URL of a script that will accept your form and send it to the email address you specify. The script is a little program on the server. You will probably need to include specific fields in your form to identify the target and originating email addresses.

The following diagram shows how the form submission process works:

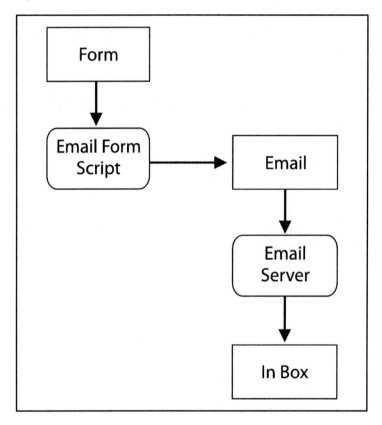

- The visitor fills out the form and clicks the Submit button.
- The Web server passes the form to the form emailer script.
- The script collects the information from the form, packages it up into an email, and sends it to a mail server.
- The mail server delivers the email to the specified in box.

Required fields in the form identify the From address, the To address, and sometimes even the identity of the mail server.

If you would like to add this type of feature to your Web site, contact your hosting company and ask them if they support email submission of input forms. If they do, ask for a working example upon which you can model your efforts. You can also get an idea of how email form scripts work by reviewing the next section, which uses a survey form as an example.

A Simple Form Example

A surefire way to get valuable feedback is to put up a survey page. A survey is just another type of form that offers a simple way to collect useful information from your visitors.

The survey is usually a Web page. It has input fields for visitor responses, and a submit button. The submit button sends the form fields to a script. The script generates an email message that is sent to the email address you specify.

To set up a survey form, use the form tools in your favorite Web page editor, or write the HTML code yourself. The HTML sample code shown below is for a simple, unformatted, survey form.

We'll use this form to explain how emailed forms usually work. Even if you don't understand HTML, you should be able to follow along and learn about the issues involved. The form asks visitors for their name, email address, a site rating, and comments.

```
<!-- This is a sample survey form -->
<form name="Survey" action="mailform.asp" method="post">
<input type="hidden" name="MailTo" value="survey@mysite.com">
<input type="hidden" name="NextURL" value="Thanks.htm">
<p>Name: <input type="text" name="VisitorName" size="40"></p>
<p>Email Address: <input type="text" name="EmailAddress"
size="40"></p>
<p>Please Rate This Site:
<input type="radio" name="Rating" value="1">I like it
<input type="radio" name="Rating" value="2">It's okay
<input type="radio" name="Rating" value="3">It needs work</p>
<p>Comments: <input type="text" name="Comments" size="40"</p>
<p><input type="submit" value="Submit"></p>
</form>
```

Now, let's look at the code.

As you can see, the action attribute sends the form input to a script called mailform.asp. The input tags define the fields. They also give each field a name, like VisitorName and Rating. The hidden input tag named MailTo provides the recipient email address. The NextURL field is the URL of the page your visitor will see after the script processes the form.

Now that you have a form, you need to figure out what script to use. Your best bet is to ask your hosting company if they have a script that can send a form as an email message. Most of them do because it is a common request.

Then plug the URL of your host's script into the form's action attribute. In this case, you'll replace mailform.asp with the URL of your script.

Every script works a little differently, so you may need to set up different or additional hidden input tags to control the operation of the script. For example, the field that identifies the recipient address may not be named MailTo. It might have a different name, though it will usually be obvious what it's for.

If your hosting company doesn't have a script you can use, then surf the Web for a freebie script that is compatible with your hosting service. By compatible, we mean that if your site is hosted on a server running the Linux operating system, make sure the script runs on Linux.

Of course, if you have programming experience, you can write a script yourself. If you don't, finding a simple, free script and testing it out is a good way to learn the basics.

Once you have your form in place on your Web site and your script is ready, make sure you test it. Fill out your form and click the submit button. If everything works properly, you should receive the message generated by the script. The format of the message also depends on the script, but it will probably look something like this:

```
[VisitorName]Nowan Yuno

[EmailAddress]bogus@hotmail.com

[Rating]1

[Comments]Informative site!
```

Whether you use your host's script or your own, remember that it is pointless to ask for information if you don't do anything with it! For this example, you would probably want to enter some of the information into your contact manager and perhaps put the ratings into a spreadsheet so you can calculate an average rating. That way you could track how the average rating changes when you make enhancements to your Web site.

A word of caution: never ask for sensitive information like a credit card number using an email form. All Internet transmissions are subject to hacker interception. Since email is transmitted as plain text, it's not encrypted. Hackers can see the contents of the message and easily rip off credit card numbers. We talk about security in much more detail in the Ecommerce section.

Setting up your first survey form can be a bit of an adventure! Once it is done, creating new forms and changing existing ones is easy.

Respect Visitor Privacy

When you create forms, you are collecting personal information from your customers so you can better serve them. That information can be used to find out what your customers want and to improve your products.

Acquiring customer information can be tricky. You have to gain the trust of your customers before they'll share personal data with you. So how can you obtain personal customer data without violating that trust?

The main trick to getting folks to fork over their personal information is to be honest! Tell them up front why you want it, what you will do with it, and what you won't do with it. The more specific you are, the more believable you will be. Develop a clear privacy policy, explain it in plain English, and stick to it.

You might be wondering why you should collect personal information in the first place. Especially since owning that information is a responsibility. If you abuse it, intentionally or not, it could cost you business. But collecting information can also help you serve your customers better.

Amazon.com understands how to use personal information better than anybody. Consider what happens when you add an item to your shopping cart. Amazon not only makes recommendations for related items, but they tell you what else was purchased by the people who bought the same item you did.

This cross-referencing of customer interest helps you identify products you might not otherwise have thought of buying. And of course, buying is the point. Is this an example of using personal information? You bet. To perform the cross-reference, Amazon.com has to keep track of everything that everyone buys.

One important thing you can do with personal information is use it to stay in contact with your customers. By keeping in contact, we ***do not*** mean spam. We suggest that you encourage customers to "opt-in" to getting regular communications from you, such as a newsletter or announcement. If you give them something they want, most people are more than happy to sign up.

Another good use of personal information is to analyze it in aggregate. In other words, collect the information, and then analyze it so you get a demographic picture of your customer. This kind of analysis is a win-win. You can better tailor your offer to your target market, and your customers get better offers.

Always remember that the personal touch works online. Customers love it when your Web site greets them by name or you send them personal emails. They are delighted when you recommend things you know they will be interested in based on prior visits to your site or prior purchases. Personalization shows your customers that you are paying attention to what they like. It demonstrates that their needs are important to you. The bottom line is that paying attention to and caring about the customer always makes good business sense.

Information Feeds

In the ongoing battle to keep your Web site fresh, generating new content is difficult. It's all well and good to say you should add new material to your site. But who has the time?

The best content is the kind you don't have to produce. An information feed can do the job for you. An information feed is a set of links provided by another Web site. The links take your visitors to a Web page (usually one that is located on the site providing the feed). The provider regularly updates the links. Beyond the initial setup, the new links automatically appear on your site without any effort on your part.

Here's an example: If you visit the Computor Companion Home page at http://www.computorcompanion.com/, you can see that we include an information feed from the Logical Tips site http://www.logicaltips.com/ at the right of the page. We also have a tech news feed at the bottom of the page.

Both information feeds work similarly. For the Logical Tips feed, we include the following HTML at the appropriate location on the page:

```
<script language="javascript"
src="http://www.logicaltips.com/LPMFeed.asp?CMD=TOC">
</script>
```

The script tag runs the LPMFeed.asp script on the Logical Tips Web site. That script generates links to the articles in the current Logical Tips issue and returns them to the browser. When a new issue of Logical Tips goes online, the feed automatically sends out links to the latest articles.

We use Cascading Style Sheets to control the look of the information returned by the script, so we have full control over how things are rendered on the Computor Companion site. In fact, you can add this code to your own Web page and customize the look with the predefined styles. Here are the style definitions we used:

```
<style type="text/css">
.LPMFeedTOCCover {color:#003399;
    font-family:Arial,Helvetica,sans-serif;
    font-size:10pt; font-weight:bold;}
.LPMFeedTOCTitle {color:#0066CC;
    font-family:Arial,Helvetica,sans-serif;
    font-size:8pt; font-weight:bold;}
.LPMFeedTOCSummary {color:#000033;
    font-family:Arial,Helvetica,sans-serif;
    font-size:10pt; font-style:italic; font-weight:normal;}
</style>
```

All of the style definition names are prefixed with LPMFeedTOC. The Cover style controls how the cover date looks, the Title style controls how the article title looks, and the Summary style controls how the article summary looks.

You also can find free news feeds, just like the one we got from Moreover.com. Adding the news feed was just as easy as adding the Logical Tips feed. Moreover.com also uses styles to give you control over the appearance of the links. We just pasted some HTML that we got from Moreover.com into the Home page at the appropriate location in the page.

If you are interested in adding fresh content to your Web site without having to do the work to create it, try searching the Web for "news feed," and look for a feed that interests you. Some feeds cost money, but you can usually find something acceptable that doesn't. Ideally, you want a feed that complements your other site content, which is why we chose tech news for http://www.computorcompanion.com/.

The next time you lament the fact that you haven't had any time to update your Web site, consider adding a news feed or other information feed and let someone else do the work!

RSS

As you surf around Web sites on the Internet, you may have noticed little buttons that say RSS on them. So now you're wondering, "what is RSS?" RSS is another type of information "feed."

Depending on who you ask, RSS stands for Rich Site Summary or Really Simple Syndication. Basically, with RSS, big Web sites that publish a lot of content can syndicate it to other sites or notify people automatically whenever they update the site.

Instead of using email to tell people new content is online and being faced with endless spam filters, blacklists, and so forth, some publishers are using RSS to give people the opportunity to read their content using an RSS reader. The content is "fed" to the readers and other Web sites, so you hear the term "RSS feed" a lot.

The concept is much like a real world "news wire" or article syndication where one article is published in many places. For example, the venerable Dear Abby column is syndicated and appears in countless newspapers.

Large content sites use RSS to republish articles or portions of articles on other Web sites. For example, the Google News site gets all its articles from many sources using RSS feeds. For online publishers, RSS is a great way to get their content seen by more people.

RSS feeds can be picked up by Web sites, but individuals can read them as well using special software. Much like a Web browser can interpret HTML code, RSS readers (sometimes called "news readers") can display RSS feeds. So instead of signing up for a weekly newsletter, you can sign up for an RSS feed of your favorite content site or blog and whenever the new newsletter appears online, you can read it in your news reader. You don't have an extra email message in your inbox, but you do need to get the reader software.

After you have the software, you can start subscribing to feeds. That's what those little buttons are used for. Click the button, get the URL for the page, and put it into your feed reader. The concept is similar to bookmarking your favorite site. Then when you are ready to read the new stuff on your favorite sites, you tell the reader to find it and bring it back to you.

As a Web site owner, adding an RSS feed to your site increases the audience for your information. Of course, the more people who see your site, the better!

Advertising

Depending on the nature of your Web site, including advertising can be a good way to offer your visitors added value and interest. Most people claim to be turned off by ads, but that's if there are tons of ads that aren't of interest. When you run across an advertisement for something you want, you may actually be glad because it gives you information that you need to make a purchase.

The moral here is to only put up ads that are relevant to your visitors. If you are going to distract visitors from the content of your site, you might as well do it for something useful to them. If a distraction doesn't add value, it subtracts value. These types of ads can even generate revenue for you, if you become an affiliate for the merchants you are promoting.

You can try to sell advertising on your site to generate additional income. Some Web sites owe their very existence to advertising sales. Charging for ad space is usually a tough sell, however. You have to offer content that is not available elsewhere for free and reassure advertisers that many, many people will be seeing their ad. Most sites that don't generate revenue from their own product sales put up advertisements instead. If you don't have a product, but you have a site that gets a lot of visitors, including advertisements for affiliate products is a good option.

If you don't want to display the same ad in the same space over and over, you can use an ad rotator. An ad rotator lets you put multiple ads in the same space on a Web page. Because the ads all occupy the same spot on the page, they must be the same size. When you click an ad you go to the advertiser's Web site.

When you are looking for an ad rotation tool, here are some common features you should consider:

- Image management features. These features help you upload your ad images, group them into rotations, and manage their placement on your site.

- Display weighting. This feature lets you display certain ads more often than others, or for longer periods of time.

- Randomizing. This option ensures that all of the ads get an equal display opportunity by randomly selecting ads. Some tools can even ensure that all ads in the rotation are displayed before any one of them is displayed a second time.

- Reporting. This feature lets you generate reports that show how many times visitors saw an advertisement and how many times the ad was clicked. You can use this information to assure your advertisers that they are getting what they paid for, or to track your own affiliate ad responses.

You can find ad rotators in an infinite variety of configurations. Some are free and some can be expensive. Currently, three main varieties of ad rotators exist:

- Client-based: These rotators are generally JavaScript code that you insert into your page. You modify the script to specify what images you want to rotate and the URLs you want for navigation. They work great for simple ad rotation needs. They can also update on the fly without requiring a page refresh. The downside is that you have to know enough about JavaScript to correctly tweak the code for your needs. Also, these scripts usually don't have many ad management features. You can find sample ad rotation scripts for free on the Internet.

- Server-based: These tools are usually CGI scripts or Web software that you install on your Web server. They offer many advanced features, including an administration interface that lets you manage your advertisements over the Internet with browser forms. To retrieve an ad for display, you insert a few lines of code into your Web page. This code retrieves the next ad from the server software. You normally have to refresh the page to see the next advertisement in the rotation.

- Service-based: Some Web Application Service Providers (ASPs) offer ad rotation facilities. These tools often work like a news feed, where you put a line of code into your Web page that retrieves the advertisement from the ASP. You use administration tools hosted on the ASP's site to manage your ads. The downside is you may not be able to pick and choose which ads are displayed.

If you think ad rotation would be a good addition to your site, talk to your hosting company. They may already have something loaded on the Web server that you can use for free (or for a nominal charge).

Google AdSense

If you've looked into site advertising at all, you've probably at least run into Google AdSense (http://www.google.com/adsense). With AdSense, context-relevant ads appear on your pages if you include a small block of code.

When someone surfs to your site, Google scans the text on the page and puts in relevant ads. If the visitor clicks the link, you get paid. If Google can't find any relevant ads, it includes generic ads for non-profit companies or your own ads.

AdSense is a good way to help make your site pay for itself if you have targeted content. However, Google has a number of restrictions as to the type of sites it accepts, so read the fine print before you apply.

For a small service business site, including AdSense ads rarely is a good idea. You are trying to sell visitors on your service, and you don't want to distract visitors from your sales message. Plus depending on your text, AdSense ads might even display ads for your competitors.

As an example, we don't include AdSense on any pages of our Logical Expressions site that talk about our services (http://www.logicalexpressions.com). However, our Computor Companion online magazine site is filled with informative articles about how to use computers, so AdSense ads often are relevant and interesting to our visitors. We have AdSense on all the article pages and it brings in a tidy amount of money. We love getting checks from Google every month!

Community Ware

If you give your customers a way to interact with you and each other online, you give them a good reason to return to your site again and again. Many software tools are designed just for this purpose, and it's likely your hosting company can hook you up with some of them. You can also search the Internet for scripts or software you can install on your site, but the onus is on you to figure out how they work (and to support them when they break).

Here are some specific examples of community ware.

Chat

Chat software lets visitors write to each other in real time. Usually the software presents two panes: one that displays the comments of the other visitors and one that accepts input from you.

Most chat software supports the concept of rooms. With rooms, you can organize the chat sessions into specific discussion topics. Sometimes you can even keep a record of the discussion for later reference.

The downside of chat is that everyone has to type his or her comments. The conversation has odd little delays and can get out of sync. Also, depending upon how you have the software configured, the participants may be more or less anonymous. Anonymity can be either an advantage (more freedom of expression) or a disadvantage (excessive freedom of expression).

For businesses, chat can be used as a good supplement to your customer service. You can give customers a chance to communicate with someone in your company who can help them with a particular question. Publicize a schedule of who will be available when.

Discussion Groups

A discussion group, forum, or bulletin board lets visitors drop by and post a message whenever they want. For example, if someone posts a question, anyone else can post a response. A series of related postings is called a thread, which you can follow from the beginning to see the entire discussion.

Like chat, discussion groups are great for customer support. Many software companies use them as a free support option. An advantage to this approach is your customers frequently help each other out. Often a customer posts a question and another customer provides the answer. It's like having expert customer service reps available for free! If you've never seen a discussion board, feel free to check out ours. We have set up a discussion board for our software, books, and content sites at:

http://forum.logicalexpressions.com

If you have questions on this book, register for the forum, and feel free to ask away! (Post your question in the special section called Books.)

Blogs

A blog is another thing that can be added to a Web site, or it can even be a Web site all by itself. A blog is basically a date-based Web site where people can add comments. The term is short for Web log. Frequently a blog points to articles on the Web with editorial commentary.

Blogs are often quite personal in their subject matter, kind of like a journal that is publicly available on the Web. The activity of updating a blog is "blogging" and someone who keeps a blog is a "blogger." Blogs are typically updated daily using software that allows people with little or no technical background to update and maintain the blog. Postings on a blog are almost always arranged in chronological order with the most recent additions featured most prominently.

Blogs have hit the Internet mainstream in the last few years; even politicians have them now. But really blogs aren't a new innovation. In fact, some blogs have been around pretty much since the beginning of the World Wide Web.

What is new is the software you can use to create blogs. Now you can use reasonably simple software such as Blogger to create a blog site without needing to know how to create a Web page or HTML. All you need is a Web browser. Other popular blogging tools are made by Movable Type and WordPress.

Because creating a blog is now so easy, blogs have proliferated throughout the Web. Literally hundreds of thousands of blogs are online covering every imaginable topic. Not surprisingly, there are also a lot of sites that list blogs (called aggregators).

From a business standpoint, the other thing you can do with a blog (once your business site is up) is use links from your blog to point to new pages and information. Basically, put a snippet from your blog entry to point to the page. That provides incoming links to your site, which search engines like. In fact, that's the primary purpose of our blog:

http://blog.logicalexpressions.com

We rarely write much on our blog because we write so much on our other sites. But we do put links in the blog entries to point to the full articles or site. Most blog software has "pinging" built in which basically notifies blog aggregators that you've posted something. Another advantage to blogs is that search engines love them.

Because they are updated often, contain a lot of content, and feature simple text-oriented designs, they adhere to many of the recommendations in this book.

Podcasting

Podcasting is a way of publishing sound files to the Internet that people can receive through a feed. Basically it's like an RSS feed for audio. The term is sort of a combination of Pod (in honor of Apple's iPod) and broadcasting. However, contrary to popular belief, you don't need an iPod to listen to a podcast.

Basically podcasts are just MP3 files, so you can listen to them using any software that can play MP3s. Sometimes it's also used to describe broadcasting video data as well, although many other names are often used, such as video podcasting or videocasting.

As with an RSS feed, people "subscribe" to your podcast. When you put it up, it appears in their "podcatcher" feed reader or aggregator that the new broadcast is available.

In fact, the main thing that makes podcasting different from just putting a recording on your Web sites is that you can publish (podcast) a show that listeners can subscribe to. People sign up to receive the show automatically without having to go to your site and download it.

As an addition to a Web site, a podcast is only useful to your visitors if you have something worthwhile to say. Many people try one podcast and view it as a big waste of time because they don't get many listeners. However, like an email newsletter, you have to work to build up an audience.

Most successful podcasts have a lot in common with an ezine or an online magazine. They are produced regularly and have interesting articles, news stories or something unique such as interesting guests or provocative opinions.

Dynamic Web Sites

The best way to keep your Web site fresh is to add new, up-to-date content. For example, if you publish an ezine, adding your articles to your Web site is a smart idea.

New content means the search engines are more likely to find your pages. It means that people who might not know about your site might run across one of your articles when they do a search. It also means that first time site visitors are more likely to bookmark your site, and return, if they can find timely and interesting information on your site.

It also means now you have to maintain a lot of content. Some of it may be time-sensitive information. As the quantity of pages on your site increases, the likelihood of having broken links and stale information also increases. Adding new information also adds an enormous administrative burden since creating new Web pages and undoing them takes time.

If you frequently update your Web site, you probably are doing one of two things. You either update the same information repeatedly, or you regularly add new information that has consistent characteristics. For example, a newspaper Web site requires a frequent infusion of articles, but all those articles have the same general characteristics (such as a title, summary, author, and article copy).

Databases are great for handling information with consistent characteristics. Using the newspaper example, you would put all your articles in the database, entering the title, summary, author, and article copy as separate attributes. Normally, with a database site you set up an administration section of your site where you can quickly add all this information on a regular schedule.

You then set up one template file that defines how every article is supposed to look on the Web. This template file contains placeholders for each article attribute. When a visitor requests that article, your Web publishing software replaces the placeholders with the actual data for an article from the database. This type of database-driven site for articles is generally referred to as a "content management system."

The database can store other repetitive information other than articles. It can be used for parts lists, business listings, or products. Shopping cart software that is used for an ecommerce site is just a specialized data-driven site. We'll talk more about shopping carts later in the Ecommerce section, but it helps to understand what the database is doing for you.

Storing information in a database has several advantages:

- The administration interface lets you update the site with no knowledge of Web development tools or HTML.

- You can take advantage of the database engine to do things that would be difficult otherwise, like returning all the articles written by a specific author or all the articles on related subjects.

- You can change your template at any time, which automatically updates the appearance of all the articles or business listings at once.

- The Web software automatically links in new pages based on the information in the database, so you don't have to worry about broken links.

New content is available on the public site as soon as you enter it into the administration interface. Many businesses have the same site update problems as a newspaper, but with different data. So an upfront investment in database software can pay off in big savings of time and frustration. Although you can certainly purchase custom software to drive your Web site, more and more off-the-shelf offerings are available that handle specific industries. Shopping carts are just one example; special solutions now exist for almost every industry.

How it Works

This diagram shows how the elements of a fully browser-based, data-driven Web site work together.

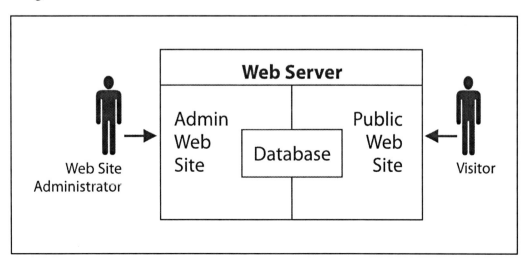

- The administration site is password protected, so only authorized users can access it. They enter information into browser forms and submit it to the server. Because they are just filling out forms, they don't have to know anything about Web page design, HTML, or scripting.

- Server-side scripts collect and validate all the information that has been submitted. When everything checks out, the information gets stored in the database.

- When visitors navigate to pages on the public site, server-side scripts extract information from the database, format it for display, and show the nicely formatted results in the visitor's browser.

Different developers take different approaches to creating data-driven sites. The next diagram shows how Logical Expressions does it:

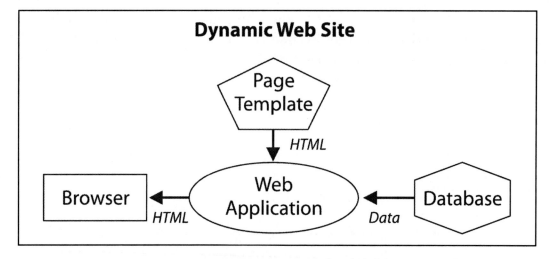

- When visitors navigate to a data-driven page on the site, a program on the server reads information from the database. Then it merges that information with a separate HTML template file.

- The template file contains data placeholders. The program "fills in the blanks," and replaces these placeholders with real data. This approach separates the HTML from the data. That way we can change the appearance of the Web page without changing the program that drives it.

Advantages

Creating a data-driven Web site is expensive because you have to pay a database developer to design the database and write the software that manipulates the database. So what do you get for your money? Here are the primary advantages of a database-driven Web site:

- Eliminate recurring Web development costs. With a static Web site, you must employ the assistance of a Web developer every time you change the information on your Web site. Not so with a site that retrieves information from a database. On a large site the time and cost savings here alone can recover the cost of development.

- Increase reliability. As Web sites grow, the potential for broken links and obsolete information increases. With a data-driven site, your links are generated from the information that is available in the database. That way bad links never get created! If some of your information is time-sensitive, you can even let the software control when that information is made available to the public.

- Increase accuracy. The administration site can enforce your business rules when accepting forms. This error checking prevents bad data from entering the system and getting onto your site.

- Increase consistency. Data-driven sites are usually template-based. The data for each kind of page is inserted into a common HTML look and feel. With this approach, you design the layout once and the system reuses it over and over again. If you want to redesign the layout, you make the changes in one place, and all pages automatically adopt the new look.

- Improve search capabilities. Information in a database is more structured than the random text in static Web pages, so you can offer your visitors advanced search features. Examples include date range comparisons, numeric comparisons (such as price less than $100), and selections based on predefined values (department, author, and so on). These searches are virtually impossible without a database.

- Work from anywhere. A browser-based system can be accessed from anyplace you can get a connection to the Internet. Your administration site lets you monitor your business while you are on the road. You can even offer telecommuting arrangements to your employees.

- Lower customer service costs. If your customers can access account information over the Internet from their home computer, your customer service representatives can focus on the tough cases that require human intervention.

- Increase customer satisfaction. Having a Web site that provides useful information and tools for your customers gives your business a professional appearance. Looking like a pro inspires confidence. Many customers would rather find what they need on your Web site according to their own schedule, rather than call during business hours and wade through a telephone menu system.

Disadvantages

Of course, you do pay a price for the convenience of a data-driven site. Here are the disadvantages:

- The software is expensive. Depending upon who you get to do the work, software development rates vary from $50 to $300 per hour. You will probably pay a minimum of $3,000 for a custom data-driven site with simple features! You can try to find off-the-shelf software that will satisfy your needs, though it can be difficult if you have very specific requirements. Even if you do find commercial software that will work for you, you do have to pay someone with the expertise to help you install it on your Web server.

- Less design freedom. The advantages of template-based sites can also be a disadvantage if you want every page to look different!

Many people have wondered how we manage so many Web sites (25 or so, as of this writing). The reason is because we solved some of these problems for our own business by building our own content management system. It gives us a certain amount of design freedom, but more importantly, it makes it extremely easy to update our content sites. As you can see, our content sites share a similar layout, but they each have a different color scheme and graphics:

- Logical Tips Ezine (http://www.logicaltips.com)
  Our weekly computer tip ezine.

- Computor Companion (http://www.computorcompanion.com)
  Practical computer help online magazine.

- Pet Tails Ezine (http://www.pet-tails.com)
  Ezine with information on pet care for adopted pets that comes out two times/month.

- Sandpoint Insider (http://www.sandpointinsider.com)
  Ezine on Sandpoint, Idaho that comes out two times/month.

- Many Veggie Recipes (http://www.manyveggierecipes.com)
  Site filled with easy vegan recipes.

- Newsletter Help (http://www.newsletterhelp.com)
  Site with articles for newsletter editors.

- Nerdy Musings (http://www.nerdymusings.com)
  Articles for programmers and other nerds.

If you think you might need a database-driven content site, check out the free demo you can test-drive at http://www.pointclickpublish.com/.

Site Wrap Up

Okay, you've probably heard enough about what you shouldn't do. So let's go over some constructive suggestions about what you should do. This section covers tips and tricks for improving the usability of your Web site.

Top Five Web Site Building Tips

Tip #1: Break Pages into Separate Tables

If you or your designer uses tables for layout, where possible, break up your page vertically using separate tables. This little-known trick can make a tremendous difference in the perceived speed of your Web pages. For example, put your heading and navigation menu into a separate table at the top of your pages. Your browser will render that table as soon as it finds its end.

This approach improves the perceived speed of your site. It also gives your visitors the chance to use the navigation menu before the rest of the page finishes downloading.

It takes time for your browser to download all of the HTML and images required to render your Web page. If you put the entire page into one big table, then the browser can't render anything until it downloads all of the content for the entire table. You end up staring at a blank page until this process completes.

Why not break up the page a bit and give your visitor something to chew on while the remainder of the page comes down? For example, you can put your site heading into an independent table at the top of the page. As soon as the browser finds the end of that table, it will render it. Follow the heading table with a menu table (if you have a menu that runs horizontally under the heading) and finally the main content table. Your visitors will constantly get feedback as they navigate your site, and they will have quick access to the menu.

Tip #2: Test Your Site with Multiple Browsers

Standards committees are responsible for defining and documenting the standards for HTML (the language that describes Web pages) and JavaScript (a language that programs Web pages). However, in spite of their efforts, Web pages are not rendered as universally as you might hope.

In fact, not only do different browser programs render pages differently, but different versions of the same browser program render pages differently. The only way to be sure your Web site works well with a given browser is to test it with that browser. You would think that visual tools like FrontPage and Dreamweaver would take care of browser issues for you. Unfortunately, it's just not the case. In fact, these tools often let you add spiffy features to your pages without warning you that those features may not work properly in different environments!

If you hire a consultant to design your pages, ask that person about how your site will be tested for different browsers. At the very least, make sure your designer tests your site with both Internet Explorer and Firefox. If your designer uses a Macintosh, make sure the sites are tested on a PC as well.

Of course, it isn't really practical to test your site with all brands and versions of browsers. So you focus on what the majority of your visitors are actually using. How do you know what browser they are using? Your site statistics will tell you, if you can get them. We talk more about statistics in the Hosting section.

Tip #3: Create a Site Map Page

As we discussed in the Web Site Content section, as you add more and more content to your site, you have to figure out ways to organize that content. Many times you need to group pages by topic or purpose. Sometimes people visit your site to find a specific piece of information. They can benefit from seeing how you have organized your entire site. You can use a site map to provide this information.

The basic idea behind a site map is to communicate the overall layout of your site. You can show the hierarchy of pages graphically, or by creating a table of contents. You can also describe each topic with an introductory paragraph and follow it with a series of related links.

If you decide to create a site map, make sure it is readily accessible from your site's navigation menu.

It's extremely frustrating for visitors to have to drill deep into your site just to figure out how it's organized! Of course, site maps are not just helpful to people, they can help search engines crawl your site too.

Tip #4: Create Printer Friendly Pages

Do you think your visitors will want to print certain pages on your site? If so, you will score big points if you create special printer-friendly pages. These pages eliminate elements that add nothing to the printed output, such as on recipe sites where you can print out just the recipe with the site framework.

You can create printer-friendly pages by creating alternate pages that contain nothing more than your site banner and the desired content. On these pages you eliminate navigational elements like sidebars, menus, links, and perhaps even advertisements. The printer-friendly page could be a link off a regular site page that shows the same content.

Yes, you are duplicating some page-building efforts. But you are also giving browsing visitors an opportunity to create a hard copy of what they found most interesting about your site. If they want to, they can still read the information online in the normal context of your site. Or they can open the printer-friendly page, print it, and save it—with your business info printed at the top—for offline reference.

Tip #5: Add Some Personality

This tip has proven helpful to many people, so we will go into it in detail. It's beneficial for any Web site, whether it's an online brochure, or a site devoted to making direct sales of your products and services.

When we put up our LogicalExpressions.com site, we included some personal information about our pets and us. Not surprisingly, our family enjoyed those pages.

What was a surprise was discovering, through our site statistics, that those pages are popular with many other visitors as well! We've gotten all kinds of comments from customers about our vegetarian recipes and dog photographs. Eventually, we took those pages and built entire sites around them.

Realistically, we probably shouldn't have been too surprised. We've read a lot of material about marketing businesses and Web sites, and we know that putting a human face on your business is important for making customers feel comfortable doing business with you. That advice was part of the inspiration for putting the information up on the site to begin with. Even so, the response was still somewhat surprising.

The fact is people want to do business with someone they know. The whole point of advertising is to get people used to hearing your name so you seem more familiar to them when they need the kind of products or services you offer. If you think about it, most advertising doesn't actually tell a potential customer anything about you. The more they hear your name, the more they think they know you!

Your Web site gives you an excellent opportunity to really humanize your company. Here are some techniques for adding that personal touch:

- Show photographs of you or your staff in action. A shot of one of your customer service reps smiling into her headset can make your business appear approachable and friendly.

- Write a brief, personal letter of greeting for your Home page. Keep it simple, and communicate in your own style. A touch of humor or charm works wonders, especially if it's accompanied by an informal photograph.

- If your business has an interesting history, tell your story. People are always curious about "beginnings." When you are first getting to know someone, you often share stories about where you were born, or where your parents came from. So do the same for your business! Tell visitors how you got started, how you overcame obstacles, and other interesting tidbits.

- Show photos of your facilities. For example, if your company makes custom-built wood-burning stoves, show your craftsman welding one together in your rustic workshop.

- Feature client testimonials. You can have a whole page of these, or intersperse them throughout your site.

- If you provide a service, show photos of you actually working with clients. (This tip is especially effective when it is combined with client testimonials.)

- Show a photo of your pets. Include a few funny stories about them. Or perhaps your company has a mascot? Share the background story with your visitors. A car dealer near here includes the owner's dog in all their commercials. You better believe that dog is on the Web site too.

- Feature personal profiles of your staff. Show off their expertise, but also put in a few personal details. For example, if one of them is a chess master, why not mention that? Include photos so visitors can put a face to the voice on the other end of the phone line.

Customers love this personal stuff because they get the chance to know you. They would rather hand their money over to someone they know than to a total stranger. Celebrity magazines are an example of this "theory of humanization" working in reverse. You see and hear a celebrity countless times on film and in television interviews.

Then, when you later read a quote from that person, don't you mentally picture and hear that person saying the words? Connecting a face and a voice to written words makes the words more interesting, and celebrity rags play that up. Take a lesson from the professional publicists who get their clients' faces in the media every chance they get. Make an impression on your visitors by showing them who you are, not just what you do.

Personalization particularly helps with first-time customer contacts. Susan frequently runs into people who recognize her from a photo that runs with the pet articles she writes for a local newspaper. That photo is also on the Pet Tails Web site (http://www. pet-tails.com) where the articles are archived online.

These people instantly share a common ground with her, so they feel comfortable opening up a conversation. They also already know something about what she is like from her writing. You can't BUY that initial level of comfort and confidence.

A word of warning: In this day of privacy concerns, a certain amount of risk goes with providing personal information. Unsavory characters might abuse certain types of personal information. Some of your employees may not feel comfortable displaying personal information on the Internet. They may see it as an invasion of privacy. They may simply be concerned for their safety.

You should be aware of an inherent security risk. Statistics show that most people choose passwords based on the names of family members or pets. If you publish that information, you need to make sure your staff is well schooled in using safer, more cryptic, passwords.

Most security experts will tell you that the real risk is not the technology; it's the people using the technology. It's the old 'weakest link' problem. It's possible to go overboard with personal information. Remember, your ecommerce site is not a vehicle for talking endlessly about yourself. It's there to help your customers and clients buy from you.

Injecting some personality and warmth into a site should always be about connecting with your customers. It's definitely not the place for venting your personal rants or campaigning for a pet cause.

So find a happy medium. Give your company a friendly face, but keep it simple. Use personal information to build familiarity and confidence, but don't go overboard with details. Give potential customers just enough information to connect with them. That information will let them feel good about buying from you.

Web Site Resources

A few of our favorite sites with information and tools for building Web sites.

Web Site Editors

- Arachnophilia (free) - http://www.arachnoid.com

- TextPad (free to try) - http://www.textpad.com

- Adobe Dreamweaver - http://www.adobe.com/products/dreamweaver/

If you have a choice, we recommend that you avoid using Microsoft FrontPage.

Color, Design, and HTML

- Color Matters - http://www.colormatters.com

- HTML Color Combination Chooser - http://www.siteprocentral.com/html_color_code.html

- Extended Web Palette - http://www.oconnor-originals.com/more_colors.htm

- Web Pages That Suck (Learn what NOT to do) - http://www.webpagesthatsuck.com

- W3Schools Web Building Tutorials - http://www.w3schools.com

- Project Cool Web Basics Articles - http://www.devx.com/projectcool/

- Webmaster's Reference Library - http://www.webreference.com

- Web Page Design for Designers - http://www.wpdfd.com

Usability and Accessibility

- Jakob Nielson's Web Site - http://www.useit.com

- AWARE Center (Accessible Web Authoring Resources and Education) - http://aware.hwg.org

- Visionconnection - http://www.visionconnection.org/Content/Technology/default.htm

Reference

- The World Wide Web Consortium (W3C) - http://www.w3.org

Getting Your Site Online

Domain Names and Hosting

After you've organized your site and created your first Web pages, you need to decide what to call your new site and where to host it. A lot of first-time site builders make costly errors at this point. So first, we explain exactly what Web site hosting and domain names are. Then we give you some tips for getting them set up based on what you do (and don't) need.

Domain Names

Once you (or your Web designer) have a few Web pages set up, it's time to start thinking about what you'll do with them. Your site needs an identity, and on the Internet, the name of your site is called its "domain." For example, our company Logical Expressions, Inc. has a domain name of www.logicalexpressions.com. Ideally, you'd get a domain name that's as close to your company name or the topic of your site as possible.

Registering a Domain

A Web address like www.yourdomain.com must be purchased through a company called a domain registrar. A registrar is an organization that keeps track of who owns which domain names and when the registration expires. When you register a domain name, you don't really own it, you sort of lease it. The registration fee covers a specific period of time, usually from one to five years. If you fail to renew your domain name, the registrar is free to lease it to another organization.

In the past, getting a domain was an expensive proposition, mostly because there was only one registrar. Now it's easier and less expensive than it was in years past. The cost for registering a domain name starts at about $10 and goes to about $100, depending upon the registrar and the number of years you want. Like the Web hosting business, domain registration has become highly competitive in the last few years. You should pay no more than $40 for the first two years of registration, even if you buy through your hosting company.

We use Go Daddy (http://www.godaddy.com) to register our domain names, although there are many others to choose from, such as www.namecheap.com. We've also listed a few in the Resources section at the end of this chapter.

We like Go Daddy because their customer service is very good and it costs about $8.00 to register a name for a year. When it comes to registrars, two companies you want to avoid are Network Solutions (www.networksolutions.com) and Register.com (www. register.com). Network Solutions is expensive and their customer service is awful. Register.com uses somewhat sleazy tactics to try and trick people into switching to their service. In both cases, just say "no."

If you go to a registrar like Go Daddy, it helps to have already made a list of names you're considering. Then you can just type in the name you want. The site will tell you if it's taken and often offer alternative names along with the .com suffix, such as .net or .org.

If the name you want is available, then you can just follow the steps to register it. Be sure to use a reliable, working email address for the contact because the registrar uses email to confirm the purchase. Unfortunately, it's getting more and more difficult to find memorable domain names that are easy to spell, so it may take a few tries to find a domain that isn't taken and that you also actually like. You may be putting the name on business cards or other promotional materials, so pick a name you can live with for a while.

When you register your domain name, you need to have a few pieces of information readily at hand before you get started.

- Contact information: The name, address, and phone number of the person responsible for the registration. Renewal notices will be sent to this person. The registrar will probably want an administrative contact as well as a technical contact, but they can both be the same person. Avoid registering your host as the technical contact. Doing so can make changing the registration difficult later on.

- User name and password: Many registrars require you to establish a user name and password that controls access to your domain names. Figure out what you want to use, write it down, and keep it somewhere safe.

- Primary and Secondary DNS servers. We explain DNS in the next section, so don't be alarmed by this acronym. If you don't have hosting yet, you won't have this information. It is usually contained in an email you get from your hosting company when you sign up. Just make sure you don't lose it. Your host is responsible for managing your domain name and any subdomains it may have (like www, ftp, or mail). So the registrar needs to know the Internet address of your Web site host's servers. That way the registrar can connect your domain name with your host.

When you register a domain with Go Daddy, you get a "parked page" which is just a temporary page that says you own the domain. To put up a site, you need to find a hosting company and pay a separate monthly fee for them to host your site. Then you can put up your pages in the space the host provides and give the registrar the new information about your site. (We discuss this in much more detail in the Hosting section.)

Some hosting services offer domain name registration as part of their service. And some domain registrars offer hosting. If you don't already have a domain name, these options may work out well. However, if your host registers your domain name for you, be sure to ask them to register it with you as the contact and to give you the URL, user name, and password required to manage the registration. You will need this information if the relationship with the host should terminate for any reason. So get it up front while they are still happy to serve you!

Choosing a Name

Most businesses should use a .com domain. This top-level domain is the most well known and widely recognized for commercial use. You may wish to register the .net version of your name at the same time in order to prevent cyber-squatting. (When someone else registers the .net or other versions of your name in order to capitalize on your brand identity it's referred to as cyber-squatting.) For non-profit entities, a .org name is often the best choice.

If possible, get a domain name that matches your company name exactly. Getting that domain may not be possible if someone else has already registered that name. If you can't do that, go for a memorable abbreviation of your business name, or the name of your most well known product. Remember that your domain name helps to create your brand identity, so you must choose something that is memorable and cannot be confused with someone else's business.

Opinions differ as to whether a long domain name should include dashes. Some search engine experts claim that if you include relevant keywords in your domain name, the dashes make it easier to get a higher ranking in the search engines. Some say the opposite.

How Domain Names Work

A number of people have asked us how domain names work. After all, there are millions of Web servers out there, so how does the Internet keep track of which server hosts which name? How does someone find your site using your domain name?

The answer is Domain Name System (DNS), which is the Internet's master directory of domain names. DNS is a system that converts your domain name to an IP address. IP stands for Internet Protocol and actually is a series of numbers such as 64.15.13.225.

All computers and services connected to the Internet are assigned an IP address. This IP address is their true unique identifier. It doesn't mean that every computer in the world has its own IP address, however. For example, when you use a dial-up connection to get your email, your Internet Service Provider (ISP) assigns your home computer a temporary IP address that identifies it while you are connected. Once you terminate your connection, your computer no longer has that IP address. That IP address is assigned to the computer of someone else who happens to dial in after you.

Your domain, on the other hand, has to have a permanent IP address because your Web site must be available all the time. So when you choose a Web host, the company assigns a permanent IP address for your domain.

If you look at a domain name, like www.LogicalExpressions.com, you see that it consists of different name elements, separated by a period. DNS organizes domain names based on those name elements. Using a tree structure, DNS establishes a hierarchical relationship between each element of a domain name.

The root node of the tree is called the null node, and it has no name of its own. After that, all the top-level domain nodes branch out from the root. The top-level domain nodes include the organizational domains we mentioned earlier, such as .com, .org, and .net. It also includes geographical domains, like .us and .uk.

Each parent domain node can have any number of child subdomain nodes. So, www.LogicalExpressions.com can be read as: the www subdomain of the LogicalExpressions subdomain of the com domain.

Curious about who manages DNS? The root node and top-level domain nodes are managed by the Internet Network Information Center, known as the InterNIC for short. InterNIC delegates management of domains below the top level to other organizations and subcontracts responsibility for some top-level domains as well. These are usually domain name registrars such as Verisign and Go Daddy. For example, InterNIC manages the .com domain, but Go Daddy is the registrar for the LogicalExpressions subdomain.

Finally, the www subdomain is managed by the individual Web hosting company. It all may seem nerdy, but when you are working with your site, it's good to know who is managing what!

As you can see, DNS is essentially one huge distributed hierarchical database of names. Distributing the database spreads the workload of finding and interpreting all the pieces of each domain name across the Internet. That way, when you type a URL into your Web browser, you end up at the correct Web site.

But as noted, the real purpose of DNS is to resolve a user-friendly name into an IP address. If DNS didn't exist, you'd have to use something like http://64.85.13.225 instead of http://www.logicalexpressions.com/ to get to the Logical Expressions Web site. Naturally, the name is easier to remember than the numbers!

If you're still confused, let's look at an example that shows exactly what happens when it's time to resolve a domain name into an IP address.

Your home computer is connected to the Internet through your ISP. When you select a Web address with your browser, your computer communicates with the name server managed by your ISP. That name server is called your local name server. It is responsible for translating the Web address into an IP address, but it may still need help from other name servers to do the job.

Ideally, your local name server will have previously performed the lookup. So it will have the results of that initial lookup cached (loaded in memory) for quick retrieval. If that's not the case, your local server must query the name servers responsible for each node in the hierarchy until the name is fully resolved.

To illustrate all the different steps required to resolve a domain, here's a worst-case DNS lookup scenario.

Assume your local name server doesn't know anything about any element of www. LogicalExpressions.com yet. Here's what happens when you type in the URL in your browser and press the Enter key.

- The local name server queries the root name server and gets back the IP address of the InterNIC server responsible for the .com domain.

- Then it queries the .com name server and gets back the IP address of the Go Daddy server responsible for the LogicalExpressions domain.

- Next it queries the LogicalExpressions name server and gets back the IP address of the SecureWebs server. SecureWebs is our hosting company, and their server is responsible for all subdomains of the LogicalExpressions domain.

- Finally, the local name server queries the subdomain name server and gets back the IP address of the www subdomain, which is the address of our Web site.

After all those steps, your browser displays the Logical Expressions Web site using the www IP address.

Here's a picture that shows visually how our LogicalTips ezine domain pans out:

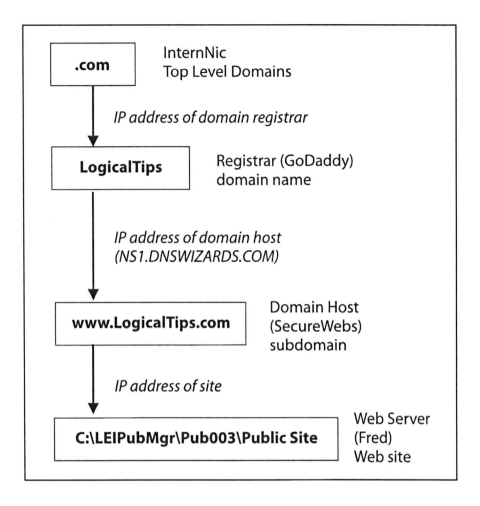

Understanding Subdomains

As you expand your Web presence, you might decide to create separate Web sites that are dedicated to your various business functions. You may also decide to offer Web-based tools or services that need to be installed in their own site. Some of these tools may even be hosted on a separate server.

However, you may not want all these new Web elements to have their own domain name. Instead you may want them to be part of the well-recognized domain name you already have worked so hard to promote.

For example, we used to have our blog (http://blog.logicalexpressions.com) and our forum (http://forum.logicalexpressions.com) hosted on a completely different server (that even used a different operating system) than our main Logical Expressions site (http://www.logicalexpressions.com).

So suppose you want to add a new Web element to your site, such as a blog. You have several options:

- You can simply put it into its own folder under the site's root folder. However, if the new element is Web-based software, you may need help from your hosting company to get it installed and running properly. The path would then be something like www.yoursite.com/blog/

- It may be simpler (or downright necessary) to set up a new site where the application can run under its own domain, such as www.myblog.com. Then you would need to link to the site from your main site.

- You may want to take advantage of a Web service that is hosted by the Application Service Provider (ASP). In that case your main site links to your instance of the service on the ASP's server, but can either point to a domain or subdomain. Our content sites work like that. The Computor Companion domain (http://www.computorcompanion.com) is really pointing to a hosted application on our server. If we used this tool to archive a newsletter, we could point a subdomain to it, such as http://newsletter.logicalexpressions.com instead.

There are pros and cons to each approach. You could register a new domain name for the new site, but it will cost you extra money every year, and it may make the relationship between your main site and the new site less clear.

With subdomains, you can create new URLs to as many Web resources as you want, without having to register any new domain names. Here's another example. As with our blog and forum, you can get to the Logical Expressions store by going to yet another of our subdomains.

When you go to Shop.LogicalExpressions.com, you see our shopping cart. Even though it's located in a different location on our server from our main site, it takes advantage of the LogicalExpressions.com domain. All we did was create a new subdomain called Shop for the ecommerce site.

The reason this works is because a subdomain is just an alias. It translates into the IP address of a Web resource. You can point a subdomain to any Web site located on any Web server if you know the IP address for that site.

How to Set Up A Subdomain

Okay, now that we know what a subdomain is, you may wonder what's involved in getting it set up.

- First, you set up your new Web site with the help of your hosting company or ASP. The host can then tell you the IP address that was assigned to the site. Note that your host may need to know the fully qualified domain name (FQDN) you plan to use to access the site. Fully qualified simply means the full domain name with the subdomain. So Shop.LogicalExpressions.com is an FQDN.

- Next, you need to contact your regular hosting company or whatever organization is responsible for managing your domain records (this is usually the same company that hosts your main site). Tell them that you want to set up a new subdomain and give them the subdomain name and the corresponding IP address. Their DNS administrator can create the new DNS record for you in a matter of moments; you may not even be charged for the service.

- You should be able to use the new subdomain to navigate to the new site as soon as the administrator enters it into the system.

With a subdomain, you can expand your Web presence seamlessly to include new sites and services under your existing domain name. You save the money you would have spent on domain name registration, and you maintain the recognition you've established with your current domain.

Hosting

After you (or your site developer) have created your Web pages, you need a place to put them. When you buy Web "hosting," you are basically just paying rent for a little folder on a computer (called a server) that is connected to the Internet. At the low end, hosting runs around $10 to $20/month and it covers the cost of keeping your site running and the bad online elements out.

What is a Web Host?

A Web server is really just a specially configured computer that runs software that will provide Web services and security features. The server on which you place your site is called your host server. The company providing that service is your Web host.

Web server software runs on many types of operating systems. Even though your own computer is probably running some version of Windows, Web servers can run other types of operating systems. These can be variations of UNIX, Linux, Windows, or other operating systems.

The server that hosts your Web pages does not have to run the same operating system as your personal computer. In fact, the operating system of your host server is usually important only if you plan to add any programming or software to your site.

If you are considering hosting your site yourself, remember that it is not a decision to be made lightly. Configuring a Web server is challenging. A mistake can compromise the security of the server and your site, as well as the rest of your internal network. Setting up and taking care of a Web server is not a small undertaking these days because of security issues, so hosting is probably not a job you want to tackle yourself.

However, if for some reason you do plan to host your own site, you must have a broadband connection to the Internet. We're not talking DSL here. If your site gets any traffic at all, you need at least a T1 line. This connection can add a major monthly expense that can run into the thousands of dollars. You must also have someone on staff (or readily accessible) who can administer the server and the Web software.

Our strong recommendation: leave hosting to the professionals. Most small or medium sized companies can't justify the cost of hosting their own site.

Selecting a Host

Since you probably won't host your own site, you have to find someone who will. Literally thousands of hosting companies exist out there. In a way, that's good. Competition has driven down the price of Web hosting, so there are many companies offering excellent value for your dollar.

Unfortunately, there is very little consistency from firm to firm when it comes to the services they bundle into their hosting plans. This inconsistency is partly because the underlying technology differs and it changes constantly. It's also partly because different hosting companies cater to different target markets. Some companies are best for small, simple ecommerce sites or online brochures. Others serve the beginning entrepreneur who is selling a few downloadable products. Still others are looking for "heavy hitters," with large sites who will have elaborate shopping carts and big databases of products and customer information.

The bottom line is that you have to shop smart. While you can get excellent value for your hosting dollar, remember that you often get what you pay for.

Avoid Free Hosting Services

First, free hosting services are rarely truly free. Providing hosting services costs money. If it isn't obvious how the free hosting company makes that money back, you should be suspicious.

Second, free hosting services rarely offer everything a business Web site requires. Most so-called free Web site hosts severely limit a number of key components such as the amount of disk space you can use. Almost all free hosts also require you to display their advertisements on your Web pages. You also almost never can set up the software or programming necessary to create Web forms. They certainly never allow the type of access necessary to set up databases, shopping carts, or secure payment systems.

Finally, most free hosting services do not allow you to use your own domain name. Instead of being www.youruniquedomain.com, your Web address will look more like this: www.thefreehostingservice.com/freespace/yourfirstandlastname.html. That long, convoluted address really messes up the memorability and credibility of your site, which reflects upon your entire business.

Select Your Web Developer First

If you aren't creating the site yourself, it is a good idea to select a Web designer or developer before you make any hosting decisions. Your developer may offer hosting as part of his or her services. This option often works out well because you have only one number to call when you have any kind of problem or question.

Your developer may use tools to create your Web site that work best (or only) on a particular operating system. If your Web site utilizes a database, the operating system is particularly important. For example, your Web site won't run on a Linux Web server if your developer creates your Web application with Active Server Pages and a Microsoft Access database.

Your developer also can help you identify exactly what types of services you need in your hosting package. Hosting companies often offer a confusing array of packages and options. It's good to have someone who understands your needs to offer input when you make your hosting decision. With this type of guidance, you can avoid paying for costly upgrades down the line or paying for services you simply don't need.

Although most Web developers will have hosting recommendations, some also say they do hosting themselves. This statement is rarely literally true. Most Web developers are not really hosting the sites themselves. They actually resell hosting, much like graphic designers resell printing. And just like the guy doing your brochure probably doesn't have a printing press in his basement, the guy developing your Web site doesn't have a server in his living room.

As noted, hosting is something best left to the professionals. Many times, when you hire a developer who hosts his own sites, you end up in finger pointing matches when there are problems. The truth invariably comes out that a separate hosting company really is involved.

With our clients, we prefer to keep the issue above board and make recommendations for hosting. That way people are involved and aware of what company is really hosting their site.

Support: The Key to Success

You can easily find a hosting company yourself. However, finding one that is reliable and easy to talk to may be more of a challenge. When you buy hosting, you obviously want a host with good "uptime" (i.e., the site is UP most of the time, not dead in the water). Uptime is generally listed as a percentage and is the amount of time that their servers are running and your Web site is available.

You may have seen articles on how to select a hosting service based on statistics like uptime. However, the best statistics don't make any difference if you can't get adequate technical support.

Often a "budget" hosting service offers many bells and whistles, but extremely limited technical support. You'll have to live with minimal documentation and technical support will probably be restricted to email communication. You also may experience a lag time before you get answers to your questions. Stay away from these budget hosts, unless you already have plenty of experience maintaining a Web site.

Your best bet is to rely on recommendations from people at other businesses who are happy with their hosting company. Ultimately, the way you are treated when you call to ask about a company's service will be a good indicator of how they will respond to you once you hand over your money. So call and ask questions.

Good questions to ask a potential Web site host include:

- How does the Web host respond to hackers, denial of service (DoS) attacks, and other security issues?

- What is their uptime? Anything under 99% is unacceptable.

- What are their "live support" hours? (i.e., when a real human being answers the phone.)

- What is their emergency procedure in the event of a major power outage or other system failure?

- Do they back up all the files on their servers, so your databases and Web pages are safe?

The hosting market is competitive. Remember, you don't have to settle for a company you aren't comfortable with. If you need a tie-breaker between two or three similar services, go for the company with the best customer support.

Hosting Plans

Most Web hosting companies offer different service packages or plans. These plans are designed to give you the services you need without making you pay for services you don't need. Every hosting company packages different combinations of features and charges different prices for those packages.

Here are explanations of the basic features most commonly offered by Web hosts.

Standard Features

- Storage Space: Most plans limit the amount of disk space your Web site can consume. Basic plans usually allow at least 100MB, which is plenty for most sites. The exceptions are sites that feature posters, artwork, or detailed photographs of products. Most hosts will sell you more space for an additional fee.

- Transfers (or Bandwidth): Every time someone visits your site, information is transferred back and forth between the server and that visitor's browser. If you have a busy site, the transfers can quickly add up. Because you are consuming precious connection bandwidth, hosts want you to pay extra if your site exceeds certain limitations. You usually start with at least 1GB of transfers. Generally you can pay for more bandwidth as you need it.

- Web Statistics: Most hosts will make your log files available to you. You can then acquire and use one of the popular Web statistics programs to analyze the logs. The best solution, however, is for the host to provide a browser-based interface to statistics software that runs on the server. Then you can just use your browser to review your statistics at your leisure over the Internet.

- Email Accounts: Most basic plans should give you at least 5 email accounts to start with and more if you pay for them. The host should give you a way to use your browser to process your email, in addition to letting your email program access it. Other things you may be interested in are aliases, which let you create multiple names for a single account, and autoresponders, which automatically reply to received messages with a predefined response.

- Email Lists: If you plan to create an ezine, discussion list, or email newsletter, you will need an email list service. The best solution is one you can manage yourself over the Internet. Some hosts bundle email lists into your package. Others make you pay separately for it.

You can also purchase third-party list servers (or autoresponders). Before paying a third-party service, see if your host's list server or autoresponder features will do the job so you don't have to pay an extra fee. On the other hand, if you have big plans for your ezine or autoresponders, you may want the features in a dedicated solution.

- Domain Registration: Some hosts will register your domain name for free. Others will charge a fee, typically $10 to $50 per year. Make sure that your domain name is registered to your company and that you are the contact for it. Register the name yourself if the host balks at this. (And now that so many domain name registrars are competing on price, it is really unnecessary to pay more than $20 per year for a domain name, even to your hosting company!)

- Chat Room: Chat comes in many forms. You can set up a chat room, where your customers can meet and discuss topics of interest to them. You can use a chat room for customer support, making someone from your organization available at specific times of the day. You could also publish the address of an instant messaging account specifically for customer service, which is another form of chat. Other (more expensive) alternatives include building chat features into your site, so you can help your customers navigate and order. Some of these tools are so sophisticated that you can see exactly what the customer is doing and even push specific pages down to the customer's browser.

- Database Support: If your Web site will use a database, such as for a shopping cart or content management system, you will need to know whether or not the host supports your database of choice. For example, on Windows servers, support for Access is frequently provided at no extra charge, but support for SQL Server or Oracle will almost certainly cost extra. Additionally, your host may charge extra for large SQL Server databases.

- Shopping Cart: Some hosts make shopping cart software available to you. The features of that software can be critical if your site involves a large Web storefront. Make sure the shopping cart software includes the features you need and supports the payment processor you choose. We go into much more detail about shopping carts in the Creating an Ecommerce Site section of this book.

- Bulletin Board: Many hosts offer access to bulletin board (or forum) software, so you can offer online support or special interest forums to your customers. A bulletin board combines the features of a chat room and email. Related messages are threaded into discussions so you can follow an entire conversation among the various participants. People who post to the board can optionally include their email address, and communicate privately as well as in the public forum.

- Mail Automation: If you plan to create online forms that collect information and send it to your email account, you will need some kind of email forms utility. Hosts often provide a script that does this, or they give you access to a software program for which you can write custom scripts yourself.

- Backup: Your host should back up your site on a regular basis, but you or your developer should also have a copy of all the files that make up your site. Backups are critical if you have a database or use a shopping cart. You don't want to lose orders.

- Contract Term: When possible, avoid signing a long-term contract. The hosting market changes rapidly, and you don't want to be locked into a service that you could quickly outgrow. Also, you don't want to pay in advance for service you may never get, if the host were to go out of business.

Email Accounts

Most hosting packages include a certain number of email accounts. This feature is essential for setting up a professional Web presence. An email address@yourvery owndomainname.com allows you to conduct business with a "branded" email account.

When you are setting out to create a professional image on the Web, branding is important. Earlier, we talked about how you should get a domain name that closely matches your business name or describes what you do (and avoid convoluted URLs like those you get from a free host).

Your domain name is one example of branding your Web presence. You should also always brand your email correspondence. For example, James' email goes out with a return address of jhbyrd@LogicalExpressions.com. Having a mail server under our LogicalExpressions.com domain name adds a little more credibility to our Web presence.

Most email software programs, like Eudora or Outlook, support multiple accounts, so you can configure your email program to retrieve messages sent to your business domain along with your personal email.

When you sign up for your hosting plan, your Web host will generally tell you the name of your email servers (usually it's something like mail.yourveryowndomainname.com). Many hosts also give you instructions on how to configure major email programs to retrieve your mail from your email server.

For simplicity's sake, most hosting companies also can automatically forward your business messages to your personal account. This technique is usually called email forwarding. The advantage to email forwarding is that you get all your messages from one place.

To maintain consistent branding, make sure your email software uses your business email address as the default return address. This way you won't be sending correspondence from your personal email address. Usually this process is simple. All you have to do is check your email software Help files for instructions on how to change the default email return address.

Don't Dump Your Online Connection

While we're on the subject of email, whatever you do, don't cancel your personal account just because you now have a business email address. Even though the hosting company gives you a new home for business email, you still need a way to get on the Internet.

An Internet Service Provider (ISP) provides dial-up, cable, or satellite services. A hosting company is different from an Internet Service Provider. The ISP makes it possible for you to connect to the Internet from your home or office computer. Once you are connected to the Internet, you can retrieve mail from any email server that hosts an account for you. The diagram below shows how this works.

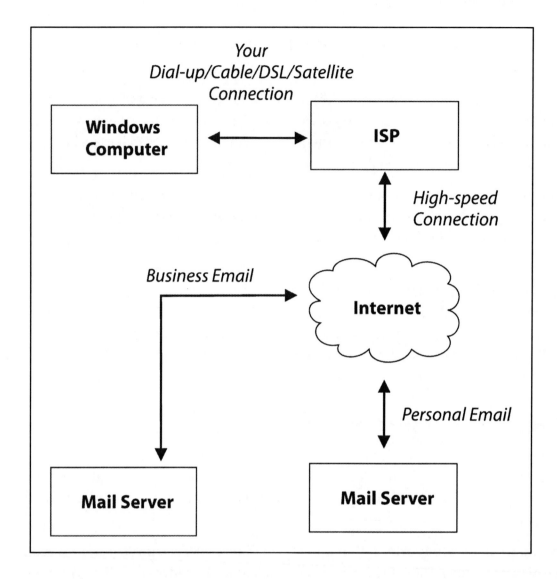

Here's what really happens when you retrieve email:

- Your computer uses a modem or other device to connect to your ISP and log on to its Internet server.

- The Internet server assigns you an IP address and your computer becomes just another participant on the Internet.

- When you tell your email program to send and receive mail, it connects to the mail host specified in your configuration and transfers incoming and outgoing mail.

- The mail host may be the same machine you dialed into. It can just as easily be a different machine in another part of the world.

As a result, you still need your ISP to establish a connection to the Internet, even if you can retrieve mail from anywhere your accounts are hosted.

What is FTP?

A question we hear a lot is "what is FTP?" Although it's yet another TLA (three letter acronym) in a land that already has too many, FTP is actually pretty simple. FTP stands for File Transfer Protocol, which gives you a hint at what it's all about. When you develop a Web site, you generally create the pages on your computer, but then you need to get them onto the server somehow. FTP is one way to "transfer" the site files from your hard disk to your Web site.

Another thing that's a little confusing about FTP is that you often hear the term used in conjunction with other terms, such as "FTP settings" or "FTP client." For example, we use a specific FTP software program (or "FTP client") to move files from my hard disk to a Web site. WS-FTP and CuteFTP are two popular FTP clients.

To transfer files to a Web site, you need to know certain "FTP settings" to access the site on the Web server. Your hosting company gives you these settings when you open an account. When you upload your files, you then type these settings into the FTP client. Usually, there's the site location (such as ftp.yoursite.com), a user name, and a password.

If you don't have specific FTP software, the ability to transfer files may be built into your Web site design software. Programs like FrontPage and Dreamweaver have FTP functions built into them.

You even can use Internet Explorer to FTP files. To do that, you put your site name into the address bar prefaced by ftp://, so if the address for your Web site is yoursite.com, you'd put ftp://ftp.yoursite.com (although this setting may vary considerably, so ask your hosting company).

A Log On As window pops up where you can type your user name and password. After you see the list of files on the server, you can transfer your files by copying and pasting them from your hard disk into the Internet Explorer window.

To make changes to a Web page, you make the changes to the file on your hard disk and then transfer the file to your server using FTP. The new file overwrites the old version with the same name, so your changes appear the next time you browse to that page.

Server Side Scripting

Another thing you may set up with hosting is "scripts." In the Web Site Graphics section of this book under "Scripting, Plug-Ins, Animations, and Sound" we discussed the benefits and perils of adding client-side scripting (like JavaScript code) to your Web site. However, the browser is not the only place scripts can run.

What's a Script?

A script is essentially just a program. The programmer writes a series of instructions that tell the server what action to take under a given circumstance. Two basic types of scripts are available:

- Client-side scripts run on the browser and control the browser's actions.

- Server-side scripts run on the server and control the server's actions.

You use a script any time you want some type of programmed response to customer input. For example, any site that retrieves information from a database or sites that accept form input for processing use scripts to do the work.

Most Web servers support some type of scripting, although the language and facilities used to create the scripts depend on the server's operating system. In spite of the fact that many languages are supported on multiple platforms, most servers are limited in the scripts they run.

You will find that Linux developers prefer to write code in one language whereas Windows developers prefer another. You need to be aware of this situation, so you can make a good match between your hosting company and your designer/developer. It is not unusual for Web scripts or applications to work on one host but not another.

If you want to use scripts on your site, be careful when choosing your Web host! Some do not allow server-side scripting. Or they may only let you use particular scripts that they have developed.

These limitations can make it impossible for you to add the features you want to your site. Always decide everything you want your site to do before you make a hosting decision. Then you can choose the Web host who offers you the maximum amount of functionality up front.

Custom Web Software

Many Web sites require some type of software that runs directly on your Web site. In fact, many software companies specialize in designing applications especially for the Web. You might want Web software to run your shopping cart and process credit card payments. Or the software might allow your visitors to make travel reservations. If you decide to sign up affiliates to make sales of your products, you might want to run software that will track their commissions.

Don't be annoyed if your Web host limits the Web software you can use with your site! Setting up software usually requires help from a system administrator and may involve an extra charge. In the end it is only fair, since they need to charge for their time.

Web software has the potential to affect the performance of the entire Web server. Poorly written software can even slow down or crash the entire server. To be safe, and to protect everyone's Web sites, hosting companies usually evaluate and select specific software products that they then make available for your use.

Host-provided software has advantages and disadvantages. The disadvantage is that you may not like the tool the hosting company selected, or it may not fit your needs.

The advantages are that you can usually get support from your host, and you are working with something that has been tested in their environment.

If you have a favorite Web software product that you absolutely must use on your site, you can probably find a host who will agree to install it for you. Plan to pay for this administrative support because it takes time.

You also must understand that you will have to get tech support directly from the software vendor. Your host simply doesn't have the expertise or time to help you.

When it is time to install software updates, make sure you coordinate these updates with your host well in advance.

If your software misbehaves and causes the server to become unstable, you can count on having the software summarily removed. Hosting companies have little patience for anything that compromises their uptime statistics.

Changing Web Hosts

In a perfect world, you would find the ideal hosting company the first time. Your experience with their service and support would be wonderful. Let's pretend the world isn't perfect, just for a moment :-).

In an imperfect world, you may find that you are not happy with your original choice for a hosting company. What can you do about it? How do you go about switching hosting companies? What are the risks, particularly if you now have questions about the integrity of your current host? There are two important things you can do to protect yourself when you decide to change hosts.

1. Avoid Domain Name Hassles
The first opportunity to avoid future difficulties happens when you register your domain name. Most hosting companies offer to register the name for you, but we recommend you do it yourself. It's easy and you remain in control of everything. A domain name commonly has three contacts: administrative, billing, and technical. No matter who registers the domain name, make sure that you are the one who is registered for all three contacts. That way, you (not your host or your developer) get the renewal notifications and any other communications from the registrar relating to your domain. We can't tell you how many people have LOST their domain name because they never got the renewal email because the hosting company or their Web developer was set up as the contact.

The bottom line is that YOU and not the host should have control over where the Domain Name System looks to resolve your Web site address. If your host retains control over the domain name, they can impede your decision to move elsewhere by making it difficult to change the name servers.

When registering a domain name, use an email address that will be around for a while. Some services make it virtually impossible to change your domain information if the registered email address becomes invalid.

If you do end up changing email addresses, make sure you switch your domain registration to the new one before you terminate the old email address.

In most cases, the registrar lets you establish a user name and password to control domain name changes. We strongly prefer this approach. If this is your situation, make sure your hosting company sets up a user name and password specifically for you. Make sure you change the password as soon as it is given to you. Be very careful not to lose this information. Write it down and lock it up in a safe place.

Many registrars also let you set up your domain to automatically renew. If they offer this option, we suggest you take it. Losing a domain name you have worked hard to promote is expensive. Plus, more and more sleazy companies are involved in domain squatting, so if you don't renew your domain, you will undoubtedly lose it. One day, you'll find a spammy ad-filled site sitting at your (former) domain taking advantage of the traffic you worked hard to cultivate.

2. Switch Before You Cancel

Get your site files moved and switch your domain name to the new host before you breathe a word to the former hosting company that you intend to leave. Why? Because it is not uncommon for a host to immediately delete your files from their server when you notify them that you are moving your site! If you don't have a backup of your files and you haven't moved them to the other server yet, you could be in a heap of trouble.

We don't mean to make you feel paranoid, but business is business, and hosting is a highly competitive, even cutthroat business. Hosts would rather expend resources on paying customers. So when they find out you are taking your business elsewhere, they may cut you loose with little thought. Your best protection is to maintain control over all critical aspects of your Web site, starting with your domain name.

Domain and Hosting Resources

A rather selective list of domain and hosting companies we know or use.

Domain Registrars

- We use Go Daddy for all our domains - http://www.godaddy.com

Other inexpensive domain registrars:

- NameCheap - http://www.namecheap.com

- Active Domain - http://www.active-domain.com

- Domains Are Free - http://www.domainsarefree.com

You shouldn't have to spend more than $15 to register a domain.

We recommend you avoid Network Solutions and Register.com.

Hosting Companies

The following Web hosting companies have been around for a while.

- Go Daddy - http://www.godaddy.com

- Blue Host - http://www.bluehost.com/ (Linux only)

- IPowerWeb - http://www.ipowerweb.com

- 1 & 1 Internet - http://www.1and1.com

- We use SecureWebs - http://www.securewebs.com (Windows only)

Reference

- InterNIC - http://www.internic.com/

Promoting Your Site

Promotion

The saying "if you build it, they will come" does not apply to Web sites. Granted, over time (a long time), the search engines may eventually take note of your pages and index them. But you can't rely on that for traffic. The Web is more like a wilderness than a mall. No one will find you if you don't put up signs that point the way.

Most people underestimate the amount of effort it takes to properly promote a Web site. Remember that setting up a Web site is a big investment of time, dollars, or both. Failing to promote it wastes that investment. Since you will be using your Web site to sell your products or services online, promotion is critical.

Before you start promoting, at least do some preliminary market research. For example, you should know your customer demographics, such as age, sex, income bracket, or any other distinguishing characteristics. You should also know if your customers tend to have specific interests or hobbies that relate to what you do.

With some basic information about your potential customers, you can make logical decisions about how to market your site on the Internet. For example, a site that sells creativity workshops may not get much traffic from search engines, so it might be better to focus on marketing techniques that get your workshops in front of people who are interested in self-improvement and personal growth. A site that sells model railroad trains could do very well with a search engine strategy, since hobbyists are more likely to search on keywords like "model railroad engines" or "toy train engines."

In this section, we give you common marketing techniques. Based on many years of working with all kinds of companies, big and small, we think you should always consider these basic, tried and true methods. Don't be afraid to explore any other marketing ideas, but watch out for anything that sounds too good to be true. (It probably is!)

Offline Marketing

When considering ways to promote your Web site, it's easy to forget to include traditional marketing media.

If you advertise in print, radio, or television, always be sure to mention your Web site address. Also, be sure to put your Web site URL on your business cards, press releases, and brochures.

We saw one very hyped "guru tip" that was simply putting a magnetic sticker with the Web site address on a car. As the site owner commuted to work and made deliveries, he also was advertising his Web site.

Opportunities like this one are everywhere if you look for them. If you have a store, put your Web site address on signs next to the cash register with forms giving people the opportunity to receive information about upcoming sales via email. Many people will happily fill out these forms and visit your site.

Another not exactly "offline" method of promotion that's effective is including your Web site in the signature line of every email you send. We are often stunned by the replies we get from people we've only communicated with once. Because we include our URL in our signature line, many people click through to our site and start reading.

Because they now know more about us and who we are, the dynamics of the email conversation change dramatically (for the better). Again, people buy from people they know. Putting your URL in your signature file is an easy way to help people get to know you!

Search Engines

Search engines are probably the first things you think of when we talk about Web site promotion. But are they really the best way to promote your site? The answer is a big fat maybe. In the end, search engines are the bane and blessing of the Web experience. Search engines index hundreds of millions of Web pages, but it can be a real challenge to locate the ones you need.

The Web is cluttered with millions of Web sites and trillions of pages. Statistics show that 97% of people do not look beyond the first page of search results. The competition for those first ten spots on the search engine results page is fierce.

While search engine registration is certainly a good idea, don't expect that to be the primary way people will find your site. Unless your visitors are looking specifically for your business name or something unique to your site, you may end up on page 6 or 6,000 of the search results. If you are in a competitive field, it's even less likely that people will find your site through a search engine.

Getting your pages placed well in the search is a challenge. Each search engine has different rules regarding the submission of pages, and those rules change frequently. Your pages will fall and rise in the ranking seemingly for no reason. Some sites, like Yahoo's Directory Submit, also charge a fee for business page submissions, without even giving you an acceptance guarantee.

If you have your heart set on ranking high in the search engines, make sure you learn everything you can about search engine optimization (SEO). You don't want to fall for the pitch of some company that promises a "Top 10 Ranking—Guaranteed!" No one can guarantee a top ranking in any search engine—at least not for all relevant searches, and certainly not permanently. In this section, we'll explain how we use a few simple techniques using good content and clean HTML code to give the search engines what they want.

Be aware that some search engines let you submit only your Home page, while others allow you to submit any page you want to be indexed. Still others employ spiders, which are automated programs that can scan your entire site by following the links between pages. You must follow the submission rules for each search engine. If you don't, you may be excluded from that search engine permanently.

Get Googled

Google has become the most popular search engine on the Web, and for good reason. It has a reputation for returning fast and accurate results with a high degree of integrity. By integrity, I mean the ranking of search results.

When you submit a search, you want the best results that match your query. For example, if you submit "wooden rocking chair," you expect to see vendors who sell wooden rocking chairs along with other information related to them, like articles and product reviews.

As described by Google itself (http://www.google.com/technology/) in addition to scanning the text in your site, the search engine relies on a concept called Page Rank to deliver relevant search results. Your site's Page Rank is determined by how "popular" it is, which relates to how many links you have coming into your site from other sites Google has deemed important. So in a perfect world, you'd have lots of high Page Rank sites linking to your site.

In other words, to get indexed by Google you need to have incoming links to your site. The Google crawler then follows these links into your site and indexes it. If you can get incoming links from sites with a high Page Rank, your odds are even better.

Google's page ranking system is pretty simple: the site with the most links coming in from the best sites wins. It's essentially a popularity contest. Google counts every link to your site as a vote in your favor. Additionally, a vote from a popular site is worth more than a vote from a less popular site.

Google runs the popularity contest (i.e., recalculates site rankings) about once a month. It takes about a month for the automated Googlebots to crawl the Web and follow the approximately one billion links they typically process. New links are added, obsolete links are removed, and rankings are recalculated. To prevent tampering, Google's ranking system is smart enough to watch for obvious ploys at faking popularity, like creating pages full of nothing but links to pump up the number of votes for those links.

Getting Indexed

So how do you get listed with a high ranking in Google? You basically have to deserve it. It isn't even necessary to submit your page to Google, because it will find your site if other sites link to it. Of course, you can submit your site. But it won't do you much good if no one else links to you.

Unfortunately, getting new sites indexed is a lot harder than it used to be. There is a theory that Google allegedly has an extra filter that it places on new sites. Termed the "Google Sandbox," some people believe this holding area keeps sites from getting good rankings for certain highly competitive keywords. Assuming the sandbox is real, it's a good reason to keep the same domain for your site. For example, our LogicalExpressions.com site has a page rank of 6. We believe that some of this ranking comes from the fact that it has been in the same place since 1997.

Whether or not a "sandbox" exists, it's irrelevant if Google can't read your site in the first place. We will go into this in more detail, but being listed by Google also depends on how the site is coded. Some sites are so search-engine hostile that Google just hits it and moves on. If Google can't read anything because the site is all JavaScript, Flash or convoluted code, you're outta luck.

In the end, getting listed in Google boils down to a few marketing basics. Just as in the offline world, your job is to let as many people know you exist as possible. In the online realm, you need to convince other sites that they should add a link to your site. The best way to do this is to perform some searches on the keywords you expect your customers to use. The sites that come back at the top of the list are ranked the highest.

Of course, it will be a tough sell getting a direct competitor to link to you. Study the links on those sites, to see who they link to. Webmasters frequently trade links with sites in related, but non-competing areas of interest. You may not get another wooden rocking chair manufacturer to link to your wooden rocking chair site. In fact, they'd be crazy to do so. But you might get a link from a site that sells cedar chests or rocking chair cushions.

When looking for links, always choose sites that will benefit from making your link available to their visitors. Make sure you are willing to give the site a link on your site in exchange. Otherwise, be prepared to pay for a link or advertisement on really high-traffic sites.

Google evaluates the content of your entire page, so adding keywords with meta tags and alt tags on your images doesn't do you any good. Some of the other search engines still use them, so including them doesn't hurt anything. But don't lose sleep over setting them up just to help your Google ranking.

A number of major sites turn to Google to power their searches, so Google is only going to increase in popularity. Until someone else comes along with a system that can compete with it, it pays to spend some time building your content and link popularity to appeal to Google.

SEO Using Site Content

Many articles on search engine optimization (SEO) focus on ways you can fool a search engine into ranking your site higher than the competition. With dollars at stake, the temptation to employ these tricks is strong. The problem is that the search engines eventually identify and penalize you for using most spider cons.

If you think about it, what the search engines really want is the same thing your customers want: accurate selection of the best sites with content that is relevant to their search. When Google launched, it became the most popular search engine virtually overnight because they did the best job of finding relevant content. Their formula was unique and effective.

Of course, the scammers eventually figured out ways to skew Google search results. And Google responded with ways to identify and penalize those scams. This game continues today and is unlikely to ever end. As a site owner, you have two choices: you can play the scam game and be stuck in an endless cycle of tweaking your site to use the latest tricks. Or you can make your site attractive to search engines by providing exactly what they want: good content. Good content is the ultimate spider bait, and it never goes out of style.

A critical element of ranking well in the search engines is having the right "keyword density." A keyword is any word or phrase that relates to the subject of your Web page. For example, if the page of this book were a Web page, some of the keywords for this page might be "search engine," "optimization," "HTML," "tags," and "content."

If your Web page contains well-written content that provides truly useful information, it will almost certainly (and naturally) have good keyword density. Many articles have been written that suggest what the "right" percentage of keywords is, but it changes so often as to be almost useless. You've probably run across sites that read really oddly. We recommend that you use your keywords naturally in your writing and avoid any artificial "keyword stuffing" in your pages. Tricks like this sometimes work in the short term, but can cause you to be blacklisted by the search engines later.

Along those lines, we recommend that you avoid the temptation of including the names of celebrities or other irrelevant words just to trap additional site hits. You accomplish nothing and annoy people who are seriously looking for content relating to those keywords. Additionally, again you risk being blacklisted by the search engines that catch onto the trick.

Misusing Tags

Many spider cons relate to the abuse or misuse of specific HTML tags. These tricks may appeal to an automated program that seeks information about your page, but they often produce messy pages that look cluttered and tasteless to a human visitor. The fact is that it doesn't matter how well your page ranks in the search engine if visitors can't stand to view the page once they get to it. If you alienate your visitors, they will learn to avoid links to pages on your site, no matter how high the page ranks in the search engine results.

If you put some thought into the way you assemble the content on your page, you can improve both keyword density and readability at the same time, without resorting to methods that compromise the quality of your page.

Prepare Your Pages

Most search engines look through your Web pages for HTML elements that give them the information they need to index your pages. Indexing is the process of cross-referencing your pages with specific search keywords, then storing that information in the search engine's database. The importance of these elements depends on the search engine, but it's good to understand what they are. When it comes to search engines, your primary goal is to make sure accurate, relevant keywords appear on each page of your site. That way, you can increase the likelihood of a match between your page and the potential visitor's search. Write your text and choose keywords based upon how you think the visitor might search for your site.

Here's an excerpt from the HTML of a fictional Web page for a company that makes rocking chairs. Even if you don't know HTML, you can still see the words just as a search engine might.

```
<html>

<head>

<title>Rocking Chair Ranch Product List</title>

<meta name="keywords" content="rocking chair,rocker,Rocking Chair
Ranch,wood furniture">

<meta name="description" content="Hand-crafted wooden rocking
chairs.">

</head>

<body>

… The rest of your Web page …

</body>

</html>
```

Remember that the HTML codes are in between the < > brackets. HTML tags often consist of a begin and an end tag, as you can see. The end tag has the same name as the begin tag, but has a slash in front of the name (e.g., <title> and </title>). Certain tags can contain other tags, as is the case with the Html, Head, and Body tags. You can tell that the Head tag contains the Title tag, because the Title tag appears after the begin Head tag (<head>) and before the end Head tag (</head>).

Some tags have attributes. The meta tag shown above has a Name attribute and a Content attribute. Attributes provide additional instructions to your browser on how to apply the tag and the information it contains. Note that the meta tag does not require an end tag because the attributes provide all of the information needed by your browser.

Hook Visitors with a Great Title

The Title tag tells your browser what to display on the title bar of the browser window. For search engine optimization, the title tag is important for a couple of reasons. For one thing, the search engines often use it when they display the link to your site. You want your title to clearly state the subject of your page so it catches the eye of people browsing search results. You also want the title to include the most critical keywords on your page, because those keywords can have a significant impact on how your page is ranked for relevance.

Use Meta Tags to Describe Your Page

You use meta tags to include information about the page that is not typically displayed as part of the content. The two most important tags, from a search engine perspective, are the Description and Keyword meta tags. These tags go inside the Head tag along with the Title tag:

The Content attribute of the Description meta tag <meta name="description" content="Hand-crafted wooden rocking chairs."> should contain a catchy sentence or two that describes the purpose of the page. Include as many critical keywords as you can, but make them part of a complete, grammatically correct sentence.

Search engines often display the content of the Description meta tag in their results list under the link to your page. The better your description, the easier it is for a potential visitor to identify your page as one that contains the information they seek.

The Content attribute of the Keywords meta tag (<meta name="keywords" content="rocking chair,rocker,Rocking Chair Ranch,wood furniture">) should contain a laundry list of keywords and phrases that you pull from the content of your page. Include the most relevant keywords first because search engines sometimes limit how much of this tag they will read. After your most relevant keywords, include synonyms and common phrases that are also related to your content.

Search engines rely on the Keywords meta tag much less than they used to because scammers have abused it horribly over the years, but you should still include it as a hint. Who knows, search engines might eventually (and perhaps already) rate sites for honest use of content and begin to trust this tag once again.

Use Heading Tags to Introduce Content

Search engines use the headings on your page as another good source of keywords. After all, your headings should introduce all of the main topics on your page.

The key is to use the correct tags for your headings (<H1> through <H6>). You might be surprised at how many site developers just use a Paragraph tag with specific font attributes instead of the built-in heading tags. That approach makes it impossible for a search engine to identify your page headings.

In general, we recommend making the page heading an H1 tag. Every section of the page should be introduced with an H2 tag. Likewise, use an H3 tag for subsections. We don't recommend that you go below an H3 unless you use font characteristics that make the subject hierarchy very clear. Conveying a deep subject hierarchy on a Web page is difficult because your visitors see so little of the page at a given time.

Here's the body of a Hello World page that includes some headings and text.

```
<body>
    <h1>Meet James Byrd</h1>
    <p>Hello world!</p>
    <p>With this page, I sound my barbaric yawp from the desktops
of the world.</p>
    <h2>Living in North Idaho</h2>
    <p>James Byrd is an Internet software developer who solves
business problems for his customers from his North Idaho home.</
p>
</body>
```

You get the idea. I added an H1 tag that summarizes the subject of the entire page. I also added an H2 tag that introduces a major section of the page.

You basically just use common sense and good writing technique as you develop your page. As you write and organize the content of your page, pull the major keywords out of each section and formulate a sensible heading with them.

Use Alt Attributes to Describe Images

Earlier, we discussed the importance of including the Alt (alternate text) attribute on your images. You use the Img (image) tag to display photos and other graphic images on your page. The alt attribute is intended to be the description or caption of the image. When you hover your mouse over the image, most browsers display the alternate text in a tiny pop-up. Browsers also typically display the alternate text in place of the image when they can't find the source image file.

We added an image to the Hello World page to demonstrate:

```
<body>

    <h1>Meet James Byrd</h1>

    <p>Hello world!</p>

    <img src="images/world.jpg" alt="Space photo of planet Earth">

    <p>With this page, I sound my barbaric yawp from the desktops
of the world.</p>

    <h2>Living in North Idaho</h2>

    <p>James Byrd is an Internet software developer who solves
business problems for his customers from his North Idaho home.</
p>

</body>
```

Some search engines use the Alt attribute as another source for keywords related to your page, which is why you often find sites that have loaded it up with all kinds of junk, rendering the attribute useless for its original purpose. This is another scammer trick that is extremely annoying to your site visitors. You may see articles recommending that you "stuff" keywords into your Alt text, but we recommend that you use this attribute correctly and honestly. It's better for your visitors and keeps your site from getting blacklisted by the search engines.

As we pointed out earlier, using the Alt attribute correctly makes your site more useful to people using screen readers. If you keep that in mind when you formulate the wording of your alternate text, you'll find that you write better and more descriptive captions. Just think about how you would describe the image to someone and your Alt text will be descriptive and useful.

More on Keyword Spamming

Earlier, we mentioned how scammers abuse tags and attributes in an effort to skew search engine results in their favor. Much of the time, this abuse takes the form of keyword spamming, also called spamdexing or keyword stuffing. The approach is to repeat all of your keywords in the text, headings, and Alt attributes on the page, thus artificially increasing the keyword density of a page.

Search engines used to be a lot dumber about this scam. They would rank relevance by counting the frequency of the target keyword on the page. Now, search engines have wised up and can tell when your keyword density is higher than it should be. Plus, they use more sophisticated ranking techniques that reduce or eliminate the effectiveness of keyword spamming.

Worst of all, keyword spamming makes your pages look awful. Visitors will see what appears to be nonsensical garbage, and they'll hit that 'Back' key quicker than you can say, "this site sucks."

You can increase the keyword density of your pages without damaging their readability or integrity. It all starts with good content. If you do a good job of organizing and introducing your content, your page naturally acquires the characteristics that search engine spiders (and visitors) crave.

If you don't know anything about HTML and you don't want to know anything about HTML, be sure your Web designer does. Just by reading this section, you know enough to cast a critical eye over the code your developer creates. On any Web page, you can right-click and choose View|Source to see the HTML. If the code isn't clean and readable and it's missing the tags we've discussed here, you need to have a conversation with your developer.

If you hire a dedicated SEO service to optimize your site, their job is to make sure that your HTML is search-engine friendly. Just be careful not to hire a firm that "blasts your site to 1,000 search engines." These firms are simply using automated submitters, and many do a very poor job. Your site may even be banned from the search engines if you use them.

Relevance Matters

Relevance is a term that is gaining momentum in the search engine optimization (SEO) world. The premise is that your page should focus on a particular topic, and the content of your page should be relevant to that topic.

Relevance isn't too hard to fake from a search engine standpoint. As relevant content has become more important for maintaining search engine positioning, scammers have reacted by contracting for volumes of cheap, poorly written "articles" that they post on their sites as so-called content. The only value these articles bring to the site is a realistic keyword density, at least from a statistical analysis standpoint. However, the human reader sees the article for what it is: junk content.

As a serious Web entrepreneur, you don't want your site to contain junk content. When people visit your site, you want them to like what they see. Junk content erodes your credibility; well-presented, relevant content builds your credibility. Quality content also appeals to search engines, because your text naturally contains the keywords that the spiders crave.

So, what can you do to create quality site content? Mainly, you just need to provide accurate and descriptive information about what you do and how you do it. If your site can answer your visitor's questions and overcome potential objections, it acts like a virtual salesperson, automatically qualifying potential leads and educating your customers so they can make an informed buying decision.

Below are a few specific techniques for creating high quality content that educates your customers and appeals to search engines.

Use Industry Terms

Every industry has its own jargon. You should not be afraid to use industry-specific words and phrases, although it might be a good idea to make sure that the terms are defined in context. In fact, a glossary page of the terms associated with your industry will help your customers while adding valuable keywords to your site.

Visitors who are familiar with your industry will search for these terms, partly because the uniqueness of the phraseology often filters out irrelevant results. Including the terms improves the odds that your site will be included in the search results.

Give Valuable Insight

When it comes to educating customers and providing relevant content, the best question to answer is "why?" If you can give your customers valuable insight into your business and your industry, they will recognize you as an expert. Even better, they might look to you as THE expert.

If your customers discover that your site generally gives them answers, you can bet that they'll be back the next time they need more information. If you can build that kind of recognition and trust, customers will bypass the search engine altogether and just add you to their favorites list. That's the best kind of positioning.

Explain

Visitors often want to understand the processes associated with how you do business. Your site should be sure to answer their "what's involved?" questions.

If you sell appliances and include delivery and installation, you should explain what will happen once the sale is complete. Explain how you will make the customer's life easier by handling everything from the moment you take payment to the first time the customer flips a switch or turns a dial.

Anything you can do to demystify your business will make customers more comfortable buying from you. If you do a better job of that than your competition does, then you are more likely to be the one who gets the sale.

The best way to identify good subjects for explanation is to consider the questions your customers ask most often about your business practices, particularly the ones where they seem wary of the answer. Your goal is to soothe fears, overcome objections, and remove confusion.

Instruct

People generally search for information relating to a question, not an answer. If they already knew the answer, they wouldn't be searching!

Your site should include as much "how to" information as you can put together. This is another situation where you should use common customer questions as your guide. The next time a customer asks you a question that begins "how do I," consider documenting the answer and making it available on your Web site.

You don't necessarily have to come up with all the answers yourself. If you carry a product that requires installation instructions and your supplier has already documented the process, then your site could just help the customer reach that information.

The best way to do this depends upon your relationship with your vendor and how often the information changes. For example, if the vendor has a PDF file that they are willing to share and the instructions rarely change once published, your best bet is to put the file on your site and let customers download it from there.

Hosting the content yourself lets you be sure that the customer can get the information regardless of whatever changes the vendor might make to their Web site. The last thing you want is for your customers to happily click on a link for instructions they really need right now, only to find the link is broken. That kind of experience stays with them and erodes the credibility of your site.

Make Information Accessible

We mentioned this idea earlier, but you can go a long way toward accomplishing the objectives we just outlined by creating a Frequently Asked Questions (FAQ) page and a Glossary page.

Depending on your business, a How To page may also be useful. This type of page contains a list of common tasks. Each task is a link that takes the visitor to a separate page with specific instructions. Once your visitors find the information they seek, they can print that page (which has your company name at the top, of course) for their reference.

Keep it Simple

Once you have great site content, the next step is to make sure you don't do anything that prevents the search engines from finding it. The best way to create a barren wasteland of a site that contains little content sustenance for a hungry search engine spider is to build a graphically intensive and heavily scripted site with lots of fancy navigation and eye candy.

Spiders want text, and they want it as quickly as they can get it. The more text in your page and the earlier the text appears in the HTML code, the more enticing your site is to spiders. If you load up your pages with kilobytes of scripting and insist on rendering your site content as graphics, search engine spiders will starve and move on.

A great Web site requires the right blend of artistic talent and technical skill from an Internet perspective. Both artists and technicians may have a vision, but their visions are sometimes extreme and contradictory. To achieve their goals, artists want complete control over colors, fonts, and effects. They tend to put everything in an image because it looks better that way. Technicians tend to produce complex, script-driven navigation and other interactive features that compromise the cross-browser compatibility of the site. Both visions have value, but they must be tempered with a consideration of the audience and environment.

You want a site that attracts spiders with pages that are optimized for the Web and that entertains visitors with an attractive layout and engaging imagery that functions for the majority of Internet users. You can do both if you keep your pages simple and use graphics, HTML, and scripting carefully.

Use Styles

One of the best ways to eliminate volumes of useless HTML is to use styles instead of font tags. Long ago, font tags were the only safe way to control how text was rendered on a Web page. Eventually, the Cascading Style Sheet (CSS) specification was developed to give designers more and better control over text rendering.

A style sheet lets you define a series of default and named styles that you can then apply to your HTML tags and control how the browser renders the information in those tags. Rather than littering your HTML with font tags, you let styles control the default appearance of the tag and override the default style with the "class" attribute when necessary. You can use a single style sheet to control most aspects of your entire site's appearance. That means you can dramatically alter the appearance of your site by simply changing the style sheet.

For example, the following style sheet causes all paragraph tags to be rendered in the Verdana font at 10 pixels by default:

```
<style type="text/css">

P {

  font-family:Verdana,Arial,Helvetica,Sans-Serif;

  font-size:10px;

}

</style>
```

Now, imagine that you need to include several quoted paragraphs (testimonials, perhaps) in your pages and you want them to stand out in bold and italic. You could add a Quote style to your style sheet that might look something like this:

```
P.Quote {

  font-family:Verdana,Arial,Helvetica,Sans-Serif;

  font-size:10px;

  font-style:italic;

  font-weight:bold;

}
```

To use the style in your HTML, add the "class" attribute to your paragraph tag as shown below:

```
<p class="Quote">The best customer service I've ever received!
Thank you!</p>
```

Adding that one attribute applies the Quote display characteristics to the paragraph. If you later decide to change all quoted paragraphs to use a different font family as well, all you have to do is change the style.

You can do a lot more with styles, but a full discussion is far beyond the scope of this book. The main point here is that using styles can give spiders easier access to your content.

Avoid Frames

Designers like to use frames on a site so you can scroll the content of the page but keep the site header and navigation visible at all times. There are other reasons to use frames, of course, but that is the most common. Regardless of how you feel about the usefulness of that feature, using frames has consequences with the search engines.

The problem is that your visitors have to land on a gateway page of some sort (usually the Home page) that establishes the frame layout and context. The gateway contains a "frameset" tag that tells your browser how to render the frames and where to get the content for each frame.

Search engines can be confused by the frameset and fail to crawl the site. Even if they are capable of following the content references, they don't maintain the frame context of the content they find. When visitors follow a link from the search results, they land on the content page without the benefit of the frame, so there goes your site header and navigation. There are ways around these problems if you insist on using frames, but the most reliable solution is to just dispense with frames in the first place.

You have to question what frames are really doing for you. Keeping the site header visible at all times reduces usable screen real estate for your visitor, who is just trying to read the content of the page. After all, they'll see the page header before anything else anyway. As for the navigation, do you really think your visitors won't think to scroll back to the top of the page to access your navigation links?

The only place I've seen frames used effectively is in highly interactive sites like browser-based administration interfaces. In that environment, you expect your user to need constant access to the navigation menu and to regularly repeat operations. Plus, you aren't trying to attract search engines or visitors to an administration interface anyway.

Use Text Links

Going back to the desire for creative control, you'll find that designers like to put all the significant site text inside a graphic. They like to use rollover images in menus so you can see highlighting when you hover the mouse over a graphical navigation link.

As we pointed out in the Web Graphics section, using graphics for navigation links has several disadvantages. It chews up extra bandwidth, making your page larger and slower to load. It requires multiple trips to the server to retrieve each image, again slowing down your page loads, and sometimes showing broken image artifacts if visitors try to use the page before the download is complete. As visitors navigate your site, browser caching often reduces this effect for frequently used images, but the initial page load can be painful. Finally, search engines can't do much with graphical links, other than follow the page reference.

If you use text links, you avoid the performance disadvantages, and at the same time, you give the search engines additional keywords to spider. The keywords associated with links are often the most important keywords on your site. The spider won't "see" any of these keywords if you've rendered them as an image.

Additionally, you can always use styles to gain a great deal of control over the display characteristics of your links. You can even specify hover attributes that highlight the text when visitors position their mouse over the link.

Another problem you will often see associated with graphical links is the use of JavaScript to perform the navigation (although JavaScript could be used with text links as well). Remember that spiders are pretty dumb: If your anchor tag uses a script function to navigate rather than a straightforward URL, that link is effectively useless to the spider. Those fancy drop-down and fly-out menus you see all over the Web are generally hurting the sites that host them from a search engine perspective.

Use External File References

If you use a significant amount of JavaScript or a large style sheet on your site, you should consider putting the content into a separate file and referencing it from the pages that use it. The advantage to using external file references is that the style sheet or script is no longer part of your page. That means spiders don't have to wade through all of that code to get to your "real" content, and your page should load faster as well. Another benefit is that you can make changes to your external file and all pages that reference it will automatically reflect the update.

The downside to this approach is that the browser must make an extra trip to the server to retrieve the external file the first time it finds a reference. The browser usually does cache the file for immediate access on all subsequent references, however. This behavior depends upon your browser cache settings. Even if you don't see a big improvement in page load performance, you've still improved the situation from a search engine and site maintainability standpoint.

Although you can use server-side includes (SSI) to achieve the same effect as an external file reference, the client browser doesn't gain any benefit, and neither does a spider. A server-side include is inserted into the page at the server, so to the browser retrieving the page, it is just as if the content of the include file were actually part of the requested page.

To create an external style sheet, move the content of your Style tag into a separate file with a .css extension, and remove the Style tag that surrounds the styles. Then, in the Head tag of your page, insert a reference to the style sheet. Here's an example of an external style sheet reference:

```
<link rel="stylesheet" href="Styles.css">
```

The above reference assumes you've created a file named Styles.css that exists in the same folder as the referencing page.

To create an external script file, move the code to a separate file with a .js extension, and remove the Script tag that surrounds the code. Then, at the appropriate place in your page, insert a reference to the script file. Here's an example:

```
<SCRIPT language="JavaScript" src="ImageRot.js"></SCRIPT>
```

The example assumes you are coding JavaScript, of course. The reference inserts the script in the ImageRot.js file, which is located in the same folder as the referencing page.

Avoid Pop-ups

The last little topic to cover is the subject of pop-ups. Pop-ups are the little browser windows that open on top of your page, usually in response to the click of a link. Pop-up windows often eliminate all extraneous browser controls, such as toolbars, the address bar, and the status bar. The goal is usually to provide some extra tidbit of information that isn't worthy of its own full page on the site. (Pop-ups are used for other, more nefarious, purposes as well, but those aren't the ones we're talking about here.)

The main problem with pop-ups is that you pretty much have to use JavaScript to open them, if you want control over the window size and want to turn off the navigation features in the popped-up window. Again, spiders can't follow links that are driven by JavaScript. Any content you put into a pop-up is effectively hidden from search engines.

Pop-ups have their place. For example, they can be very useful for displaying quick definitions of highlighted words in your content. Just make sure that the definitions also exist on an FAQ or glossary page elsewhere on your site so the spiders can find the definitions as well. On the other hand, most people hate pop-ups and have some type of "pop-up killer" software installed to avoid seeing them.

It's Your Choice

If you care more about the appearance of your site than its ability to be found by the search engines, then by all means, feel free to use all the fancy tools in your kit. If, however, you want to optimize your position in the search engine rankings by virtue of your site's content, then follow the techniques and recommendations we've outlined. Not only do the techniques work, they never go out of style. Our sites have ranked well in the search engines for almost 10 years now thanks to quality content and clean code.

If you want the search engines and your visitors to love your site, then make it the prime destination for anyone seeking information in your industry by providing volumes of high-quality, relevant content. Then, avoid site features that damage the accessibility of that fabulous content.

As the Web evolves, the rules of the road change regularly, making the job of creating a successful Web site more challenging all the time. That is one reason why we recommend that you stick with the basics and always remember that the goal of a Web site is to deliver information to people in an accessible format.

HTML and text are the fundamental building blocks of Web content, and anything you do outside of that realm, whether it's Flash, excessive graphics, or JavaScript, has a price in terms of compatibility with search engines and browsers. You want your site to be around and working for your business for the long haul, so just avoid any scammy tricks.

Do SEO Right the First Time

The reason we stress search engine optimization using clean code and good content is because it's expensive to redo sites. Many of the Web design jobs we've done are for "second generation" Web sites. We've seen what happens when a Web site is not done right the first time.

The sad reality is that we've made a lot of money redoing Web sites that were utter failures for one reason or another. Our clients realized that "search engine optimization" isn't just a buzzword. Search engines are way smarter than they used to be and sleazy old tricks don't work any more.

Our clients realized that they needed a site that people can actually find by searching online. From a business standpoint, a site no one can find may as well not even exist. It's certainly not doing you any good. Our clients were dismayed to find that the "cool neat-o" site they were talked into was totally search engine hostile, and called us in to redo it with SEO in mind.

We did one database site for a real estate company where we were the *third* Web development company to work on it in the prior year. The site was so ugly and hard for them to maintain, it was sickening. To say that the client is happy now with their new site is a radical understatement. Real estate is competitive these days and prospective clients now can find their company online.

Unfortunately, in every site redesign case, we had to throw away virtually everything but the text and pictures because the underlying site code was garbage. But our clients have been thrilled with the results. After all, a Web site no one can find is an expensive waste of time. But a Web site that works is worth every penny you paid for it.

Linking Campaigns

As we mentioned in the Get Googled section, having incoming links to your site is important. You can encourage more links and increase the value of your site by creating a links page that provides links to other sites of interest to your customers.

For example, if you sell appliances, you might include links to the Web sites of the manufacturers you carry. You can also include links to other businesses that sell related products that don't compete with yours.

It is considered good form to let those businesses know that you would like to link to them. They may return the favor and put a link to your site on their links page. These reciprocal links can help drive more traffic to your site, which in turn can raise your Google page rank. At the very least, reciprocal links provide useful information to visitors of both sites, raising your credibility and increasing the odds of return visits.

Unfortunately, linking is another thing that is subject to abuse. Because our sites rank highly, we constantly get requests to link to other sites. In almost every case, the email is obviously a canned letter and the author never even looked at our site. The person requesting the link is generally requesting it for some sleazy site that we'd want nothing to do with, such as spam sites like online casinos, drugs, and so forth. Google and other search engines actually penalize sites for including links to "bad neighborhoods" and spammy link pages with links to unrelated, irrelevant sites.

If you decide to contact other site owners for links and sincerely think they'll add value, many people will give a link back to you. For example, our IdeaWeaver software site (http://www.IdeaWeaverSoftware.com) has a link page with links to all the download sites that have our software available.

In this case, the links are relevant. The sites are linking to our site and it makes sense for us to link to these sites, so our users have a convenient list of all the places they can download the free trial of IdeaWeaver.

A more recent hybrid of the linking campaign is the "article campaign." If you are a prolific writer, this approach can work well. Basically, you write articles and submit them to one of the *hundreds* of article directories out there in cyberspace (we've only included the biggest one in the Resources section because they are multiplying like bunnies). These articles are free for anyone to use online, as long as they include your biographical information and a link back to your site.

The idea is that you get tons of incoming links to your site. The bad news is that this technique is not without risks. We recommend that you not use articles that you have on your own sites because as usual the search engines have caught on. There is a possibility that they will (or already have) imposed a "duplicate content penalty." For example, Susan has some articles on free article sites, but they aren't published on any of our own Web sites.

A related technique is to use incoming links from press release sites to increase your traffic and page rank. Basically, instead of just writing a press release and sending it to your local newspaper, you submit it to one of the big PR sites (a list is in the Resources section). Generally, to get good exposure, you need to opt for one of the paid plans. But you get valid incoming links from a highly ranked site, which is a good thing.

Submitting Pages

Submitting your Web pages to the search engines is boring and frustrating and possibly not a good use of your time. As we mentioned earlier, each search engine has different rules for submission and the rules change frequently. Some search engines even charge money to list your site.

To ease the pain, high-end software products like Web Position can help you submit your pages and evaluate your current position in the various search engines. If you plan to handle the process yourself, getting specialized software is probably a good idea. We have never used submission software, however. Because the rules change so often, it's difficult for the software to keep up. And as noted, you don't want to end up blacklisted by the search engines.

If you are serious about search engine placement but don't have the time to manage it yourself, consider hiring the services of a company that specializes in this activity. Submission companies vary in their service offerings. Here are some of the features to look for:

- Web page optimization: They update your Web pages with the elements that engine spiders like.

- Keywording: They help you come up with keywords that increase the chances of your site appearing in search results.

- Submission: They take care of submitting (and resubmitting) your pages to search engines and deal with the variations in the submission rules.

All these services cost money, of course! You can expect to pay a minimum of $25 to $50 per month, depending upon the level of service you need. That expense could be worth it when you consider how much of your own time you would have to spend to submit pages yourself.

While every promotion should address search engine placement, you shouldn't rely solely on search engines. Search engine promotion has a couple of problems.

First, no matter how well you are placed, you are still one member of a crowd. Even if you are ranked number one, nine other sites appear right below yours, all competing for visitor eyeballs.

Second, it can be hard to get qualified leads from search engines. It may be difficult to settle on just a few keywords your best potential customers will use. In fact, in some industries, it might be impossible to target good keywords at all.

Site Conversion and Incentives

So far, we have concentrated on what you can do to promote your Web site externally. By externally, we mean getting visitors to come to your site from elsewhere. So what do you do once the visitor reaches your site? How do you make visitors stay, and how do you get them to buy from you or sign up for your newsletter?

Converting customers from a visit to a buy can be challenging. You may not realize it, but your Web site may be haunted by the ghostly virtual remains of abandoned shopping carts that never made it to checkout. It's a fact, that on most ecommerce sites most visitors never make it to the payment page.

On a given page, whether it's a shopping cart product page or an article page, you probably have a "desired response" from the visitor, whether it's signing up for a newsletter or buying a product. The way you design your site and present your offerings has a tremendous impact on your conversion ratio (buyers divided by visitors).

Some of the things you should do to improve your conversion ratio are common sense. We urge you to revisit these issues frequently, and make sure your site is still doing the best that it can to convert visitors.

Make It Easy

When they are shopping, customers care more about where they are going than where they've been! So put yourself in your customer's shoes.

If they already know what they want, they should be able to find it and buy it with as few clicks as necessary. If the visitors want to browse, make it easy for them to navigate to any area of your Web site with a minimum of clicking to back out and drill down. Once again, your initial site goals and bubble diagrams are important! Before you even have a site, you'll be able to see how many clicks it takes to buy something.

Cross-Sell And Up-Sell Your Products

Sometimes you learn something valuable about the interests of your customers when they buy a particular item. So take advantage of that knowledge. Offering related items, usually at the time of purchase, is called cross-selling. Following up an initial sale with an offer for a more expensive or more elaborate product is called up-selling.

Here is an example of a cross-sell opportunity. Customers who buy an inflatable kayak from you may need additional gear, like a dry-bag, neoprene boots, and gloves. You could cross-sell the bag, boots, and gloves by placing links on the inflatable kayak page. You could even offer a discount if the extra items are purchased at the same time.

Alternatively, you could set up starter packages that discount a group of related items needed by the novice, and offer them as part of a cross-sell. Later, you can send a follow-up email with an up-sell. You would contact these same customers in a couple of months, and send them an offer for a top-of-the-line fiberglass kayak and cross-sell it with a two-week guided kayak expedition.

Offer Coupons

Normally you hear about using coupons to lure customers to your site. Why not give them a coupon for getting there as well? Copy the grocery stores that put coupon flyers by the entrance so customers can use them immediately. Customers appreciate the convenience and it gives them an immediate incentive to buy.

By the way, always put an expiration date on a coupon to give it some urgency, even if you plan to reissue a new one the next day! Also, vary the amount of the coupon or restrict how it can be used. Let customers know it might be a while before they can get the same deal again.

Reward Repeat Customers

You should periodically review your sales figures as a regular part of your marketing strategy. You should know who bought what from you and how much they spent. If you have this information, you can approach your best customers with special offers. It may mean sending them a store coupon via email, or maybe giving their account a permanent preferred customer discount.

Stay in Touch

Let your customers hear from you regularly. You should not send unsolicited email, but you should give them plenty of opportunities to opt-in. You should offer an email newsletter with at least one article of information that is useful to your customers. Your e-newsletter also lets you send current news about your company, your Web site, and your products. (We'll talk more about the ins and outs of ezines later.)

If you are out-of-stock on a particular product, your customers should be able to request email notification for when it becomes available again. This kind of follow-up always generates customer loyalty, and that means repeat business.

Even if these specific techniques aren't appropriate for you or your business, the idea here is to improve communication with your customers. Minimize your visitors' frustrations with your site, and maximize their opportunities to buy.

It is always easier to sell to customers who have purchased from you previously than it is to sell to those who don't know who you are. So give repeat customers good incentives to come back, and prove to them that you want their business.

Affiliate Programs

An affiliate program offers individuals and companies an incentive to direct traffic to a company Web site. For example, Amazon.com has an affiliate program that gives you a percentage of each sale that results from a link originating at your site. You can think about affiliate programs in two ways: as the company receiving the incentive or as the company offering the incentive.

The trick to being a good affiliate and increasing the likelihood of a sale is to offer affiliate products that are relevant to your customers. For the Amazon.com example, you might locate books that are relevant to your business and add links to those pages from your site. Your customers benefit from your pre-screening, and you benefit from the incentive.

What if you want to pay affiliates to send you traffic or make sales? You could set up your own affiliate program, which means you need a way to detect the origin of a sale. Usually sales are tracked by assigning each affiliate a unique identifier that is added to the end of their link URL. If you accept orders online, you need a way to associate the affiliate identifier with each order, so you know who to pay.

For example, we have an affiliate program for our IdeaWeaver software product. People can learn about and sign up for the affiliate program at http://www. IdeaWeaverSoftware.com/affiliates.htm. Then every time a copy of the software sells using their link, we pay them a commission. Don't worry about "giving away money" in affiliate commissions. Even if you make less on the sale, you are getting a new customer, which has value too.

An alternative to setting up your own program is to use someone else's. A number of third-party affiliate program firms promote your products through member publishers for a percentage of the sale. Commission Junction, Link Share, and ClickBank are examples of these types of programs. As an affiliate, you can sign up for programs at the sites, and as a merchant you can use them to manage your program.

It is beyond the scope of this book to tell you all the ins and outs of generating revenue from affiliate programs. However, you'll find links to sites with more information in the Resources section.

Ezines

As we mentioned in the hosting section, an ezine is an electronic magazine or newsletter you send to subscribers via email. An ezine helps keep your business name in the forefront of your subscribers' minds. It gives you an opportunity to demonstrate your expertise and inform your subscribers on issues important to them.

This type of email marketing might sound like spam, but as long as you let customers control when they subscribe and unsubscribe, it is not. In fact, because your subscribers control their participation in your marketing campaigns, a whole new set of buzzwords are now associated with this method.

In some circles it is called permission-based email marketing. Other words for it are opt-in email or opt-in marketing. Your subscriber list is called an opt-in list. The opt-in part means that your subscribers have actually requested that you send them information via email. In other words they've opted in to receiving information from you.

Sometimes the software to manage an ezine is basically a special form of discussion list where the discussion is one-way. You set up a link on your Web site that lets visitors subscribe and unsubscribe from the list. When you are ready to publish the next edition of your ezine, you send it as an email to the list server, and the list server automatically resends that message back out to all your subscribers.

Contact your hosting company for pricing and information on setting up a list server for an ezine. Most hosting companies offer list servers for an extra charge. Setting up a list server can be confusing, so don't be afraid to ask for help. Once it is configured, you don't usually have to do much with it.

Another option is using a third-party list server or autoresponder. These services have become popular in the last few years because they are often user-friendly and simple to set up. Plus, with all the problems with spam, getting your email delivered is becoming increasingly difficult. A third-party service can work with big ISPs like America Online and MSN to make sure your email gets delivered.

Some tools offer enormous flexibility. Many let you set up unlimited campaigns and different subscriber lists. Some even allow you to store and send unlimited messages in both HTML and plain text formats. A few can send audio or other types of files to your subscriber list. We've listed a few reliable list services in the Resources section.

What are the essential elements of a list server? Each one works a little differently, but they have many common features. Here are a few things you should consider when you set one up:

- Automated subscribe/unsubscribe requests. You can use a simple Web form on your site that accepts an email address and visitor name. The Web form formats and submits a message to the list server asking it to subscribe or unsubscribe the visitor.

- Turn off list probing. Some list services accept requests to report the current list of subscriber addresses. Spammers just love to find list servers that willingly give up these addresses. Lock this feature down: you don't want your subscribers getting spammed.

- Allow subscribers to subscribe and unsubscribe themselves. You may have legitimate reason to restrict subscribe requests, but you should always allow subscribers to unsubscribe.

- Use double opt-in. The subscriber gets a verfication email with a link that must be clicked for the email address to be added to the list. Double opt-in avoids getting bad email addresses into your list and verifies that the sender really authorized the subscription.

Be prepared to spend some time managing the list if the tool doesn't handle bounces automatically. For years, when we sent out one of our weekly ezines, we'd get about a dozen bounces that we had to deal with. In other words, the subscriber's address was unreachable for some reason.

An email may bounce for a number of reasons. The subscriber may have closed the account or in many cases, the subscriber just typed his or her email address incorrectly during the subscription process. Other times, the receiving mail server rejects the message because the subscriber's mailbox is full. Deleting email addresses from your list that come back from "unknown" accounts is probably fine, but you may want to let "undeliverable" and "mailbox full" accounts have a second chance.

If you decide to establish an ezine, you should take it seriously. Decide on a manageable publishing schedule. Then stick to it. Your subscribers will view the way you manage your ezine as an example of how you manage your business affairs in general. So provide quality content on a regular schedule. The worst thing is an unreliable ezine that shows up erratically, or once and never again. Like a magazine, an ezine is called a periodical for a reason.

It doesn't matter if your ezine is short. You must be consistent and provide good content.

Our Logical Tips computer tips ezine (http://www.logicaltips.com) goes out weekly. We've been publishing it since 1999, providing a small, focused amount of high-quality information. Now we publish two other ezines as well on pet care (http://www.pet-tails.com) and the Sandpoint, Idaho area (http://www.sandpointinsider.com). These ezines came about because we got so much feedback on the non-computer part of our Logical Tips newsletter.

Our newsletter subscribers remain loyal, and look forward to every issue, because they know they can rely on it. If you must choose between a long ezine published infrequently or a short ezine published more frequently, go for frequent and consistent!

Build a Subscriber Base

Although an ezine helps increase awareness of your business, don't expect miracles. It takes time to build a subscriber base, even if your content is excellent. Remember, you are much better off with 1,000 loyal subscribers who love your ezine and your products, than 10,000 subscribers who trash it without reading it.

You can increase your subscriber base in a number of ways. Encourage readers to recommend your ezine to their friends. Provide incentives to subscribers by offering them special offers or occasional freebies. For example, we offer a PDF of keyboard shortcuts to our Logical Tips subscribers when they sign up. You also might solicit guest articles if you want more variety.

Although the primary goal of an ezine is to increase awareness of your business and stimulate sales, sometimes you can earn more direct revenue by selling advertising in your ezine to other companies. Just be careful not to let the advertising overwhelm your content.

If you do a good job of keeping your subscribers happy with ethical list management and interesting content, your subscribers will remember. Not only will they tell others about you, they'll also think of you first when they need help in your area of expertise or a product that you sell.

Discussion Groups and Autoresponders

With a newsletter or an ezine (like our own LogicalTips), only the list owner can post messages to the list. However some list servers can also be set up as a discussion group. With a discussion group, you let the subscribers post messages. These messages are then distributed back out to all the other subscribers on the list.

If you host a discussion list, be sure to let subscribers receive messages in digest form. This way, they can avoid receiving an endless stream of continuous messages all day long. The digest appends all the messages for a specific period of time into a single message for distribution.

Email newsletters and discussion lists are both great ways to promote your business. The newsletter reminds your subscribers you exist. It also lets you send subscribers notices of sales and new products. A discussion list helps create a sense of community among your subscribers. The list keeps people interested in your industry and your services. The more you participate in the discussion, the more you establish yourself as an expert in your field.

Autoresponders

An autoresponder is another special type of email service that automatically responds to email that is sent to it. Your hosting company may provide autoresponders as part of your email service, or you might need to use a third-party solution.

With an autoresponder, you can set up a marketing or information message that goes out at a particular interval to anyone who subscribes or emails a particular address. It may be just one message or many messages. For example, suppose you set up a message that contains detailed information regarding your products or services. You could then set up an autoresponder so that if a prospect sends a message to productinfo@mydomain.com, the autoresponder automatically responds with your product information. Autoresponders are a great productivity tool because they save you from having to personally answer repetitive inquiries.

You also can use an autoresponder to send out a series of messages. In this case, you set up the messages you want to send and configure the timing of those messages (such as once per week, month, whatever). This approach lets you send out a series of related messages in a specific sequence over time.

The line between an autoresponder and an ezine gets a little blurry at this point, because the people who sign up for the autoresponder are effectively "subscribed" to the subsequent messages. One difference is that the subscribers always start at message 1 and progress to the last message in your series, as opposed to an ezine where the subscriber jumps into an ongoing newsletter at the latest issue.

Another thing that makes it confusing is that many autoresponder services have the ability to work as a list server as well. For example, after many years of sending out our newsletters using our own mail server, we switched to using a service called AWeber. With AWeber you can set up what they call a "broadcast email" to your list. We use this function for our newsletters.

However, they also let you set up a traditional follow-up autoresponder. We use this function to send the thank you email that gives new subscribers their freebie. And on our new VeganSuccess.com recipe book site, we use an AWeber autoresponder to send out our sequence of "10 Tips to Help You Get a Vegan Meal on the Table Fast."

Both ezines and autoresponders are great ways to remind people you exist. However, if you set up a series of messages, be sure to give your subscribers a way to unsubscribe. This capability is just as important for an autoresponder as it is for a newsletter. Remember: to avoid being considered spam, you must always give the reader a way to opt-out of your messages.

Don't Spam

When it comes to the subject of email marketing, no discussion would be complete without mentioning the perils of spam. At all costs, you must steer clear of companies that:

- Sell millions of email leads for extremely low prices.

- Send bulk email solicitations.

- Sell CDs full of email addresses.

Why? Because all of these companies are spammers!

Okay, so you might be wondering, what's the big deal? After all, how different is it to get a piece of junk mail in your mailbox versus getting a piece of junk email in your inbox? Not much, really—on the surface. Both are annoying. But at least you know the company reaching you through your physical mailbox had to spend some real money to do so. They are somewhat less likely than the spammer to be a fly-by-night scam artist.

More importantly, we have never spoken with anyone who likes spam. Some people have very strong negative feelings about spam and would like to hurt the people who send it. If we had an easy way to record the name of every company who sent us spam, we would make an effort to boycott those companies.

The problem is spam continues to make money for somebody. Either recipients are buying products via spam, or at the very least, the companies that sell spam services are making money by selling lists of email addresses!

Spam will only go away when the cost of sending it outweighs the income generated from it. The best way to wage your own battle in the war against spam is to refuse to do business with any company who sends it. Never respond to spam, even if you are interested in the product or service it advertises. You are just making the problem worse.

It's Just As Gross In Your Inbox

From a business perspective, spam is just about the worst marketing technique you could engage in for many reasons.

- Spam is completely untargeted. You have to send a whole lot of spam to make sales. Of course, the companies that sell spam-mailing services love this, since it means you have to keep buying their mailing lists over and over again. In all our years of doing business on the Web, we have never heard of a Web entrepreneur who actually got quality leads or substantial sales from bulk email.

- Spam destroys customer trust and actively turns people against you. Those people have friends that they will turn against you too. It just doesn't make sense to use spam when there are so many other alternatives available to you. In a nutshell, spam is really bad PR for your company.

- Spam is the medium of choice for the sleaziest Web businesses. Online pornographers and hate organizations have to resort to spam, since they can't advertise through legitimate means. Before you give in to the temptation to spam, remember that you will be judged by the company you keep.

Does this mean email is a bad marketing medium? Absolutely not! Plenty of highly respected opt-in newsletters include advertising. We include advertising for our products in our newsletters and no one has ever complained.

Why? Because the marketing messages are not the only thing they get. Readers like the useful content we provide in our ezines. They want to read our writing, so they opted in to receive it. Most importantly, they can remove themselves from the list whenever they wish.

This element of choice distinguishes spam from responsible email marketing. If your recipients opt-in, you are not spamming them. It has been proven, over and over, that customers will even sign up for pure advertising content! They do not mind receiving advertising if it is relevant to their lifestyle and purchasing decisions, as long as they requested it. The key is to make sure the customer is in charge of the information flow.

As an aside, our apologies to those of you out there who actually love the Spam food product. You probably still consider spam in your inbox gross, even if Spam on your plate is yummy!

Site Personalization

One of the biggest advantages of a bricks-and-mortar business is the personal touch. When you walk in the door, you see a familiar face that smiles back at you and may even greet you by name. Dealing with a person allows you to ask questions like, "Do you have something that can help me do (whatever)?"

The problem with many business Web sites is that you have to already know what you are looking for. You also must be willing to navigate around the site to find the things that interest you. On an ecommerce site for example, the larger the catalog, the more difficult the search situation becomes for shoppers. Products may be organized into categories or isolated by characteristics such as "recent release." The way the catalog is organized often does not really reflect the specific interests of shoppers.

Enter the latest trend in Web site development: personalization. The idea behind personalization is to customize your site to reflect the interests of your customers. You can customize your site by showcasing the products your customer are most likely to want, and by showing your appreciation for their repeat business.

The first step in successful personalization is to identify the visitor. Often identifying visitors is performed by storing a browser cookie on the visitor's computer. This little file stores their identity between browser sessions.

 A cookie is essentially a tiny file of information that is sent to the server by your browser. If you've ever been to a site that immediately welcomes you back by name, you can bet the site used a cookie to do it.

Cookies do add overhead to every communication between the browser and the Web server. Make sure your cookies only store information that is necessary. Typically, it's enough if the cookie just provides the visitor's identity. Then you can store any other information you need about the visitor on the Web server.

Once you've identified the customer, you can customize their experience at your Web site with some of the following personalization techniques:

- Recommend products and services based on past purchases. Your customers give you valuable insight into their interests every time they buy from you. So use that information to highlight the items in your catalog they are most likely to want.

- Recommend products and services based on other customer purchases. Similar purchasing patterns generally indicate shared interests. You can recommend items to your customers based on what other customers have bought in common with them. For example, if a lot of customers who bought a lawn mower also bought a set of ear protectors, then recommend ear protectors to all your lawn mower purchasers.

- Preserve a wish list. Customers may be interested in a product they just aren't ready to buy at the moment. Rather than make them wade through your site to find that item again, let them put the item on a wish list they can readily access on their next payday.

- Let your customers review and rate your products. This idea sounds risky because you may be afraid your customers could say something bad. Realistically, any kind of feedback is valuable to you and to your other customers. So let your customers help you fine-tune your product line.

- Offer preferred customer discounts. Once you are closely tracking and comparing purchases, single out your best customers for special treatment. You can offer coupons via email or even periodic storewide discounts.

The main problem with implementing personalization is that it requires extensive support. You have to track all the information necessary to personalize your site. That information has to be stored somewhere. Then you need advanced site programming to build dynamic, custom responses for each customer.

The good news is that more and more ecommerce solution providers and shopping cart software products offer these features at a lower cost than ever before. Ask for this kind of functionality up front, and you may be pleasantly surprised to get it without spending an exorbitant amount of money.

If your site can learn the interests of your customers, it can anticipate their needs, much like your favorite salesperson does.

Pay Per Click

Pay Per Click advertising (or PPC) is exactly what it sounds like. You sign up for a service that puts your ads up on Web sites. When people click the link, you pay a specified amount. Generally PPC advertising is found on large sites, ad networks and search engines.

When you go to Yahoo or Google and do a search, those "sponsored results" are ones people paid to have displayed. Basically, as an advertiser, you bid on keywords or phrases that have something to do with what you are trying to sell. When a visitor searches for that phrase, the advertiser links appear on the page in order of bid amount. As with regular "organic" searches, if you don't come up on the first one or two pages, you are unlikely to be found at all.

Unfortunately, PPC has become extremely competitive and expensive. Many tools are available to help you find keywords and manage your advertising campaigns. The details are way beyond the scope of this book, but the bottom line is that if your cost per click for the keywords that relate to your product or service is high, PPC may not be a particularly good option for you. Spend some time looking at the costs before you jump in.

Recently, PPC also has been marred by a practice referred to as "click fraud." In this case, automated systems or even people hired in other countries, click links not because they are interested, but to manipulate the system. Bid amounts are artificially inflated and the order of listings can be changed because of this practice. Unscrupulous businesses have been known to engage in click fraud to drive prices up until a keyword becomes too expensive for the competition.

Get Information with Web Statistics

Testing is one of the great keys to marketing success. Savvy marketers test a marketing idea, and keep refining it over time based on the results. With the Internet, testing is far easier than in other mediums like direct mail, which involve expensive printed materials. If you have a Web site, your Web server keeps track of everyone who visits. You can change things about your site, see what happens in your statistics, and then change it again.

A lot of hoopla is associated with analyzing Web statistics. Most hosting companies provide basic Web statistics as a matter of course, but some third-party vendors provide software that can track extremely detailed Web site activity.

What exactly are Web statistics? As visitors retrieve pages from your site, the server records that activity in a log file. Most hosting companies let you access your log file. This file gives you useful information about who is accessing your site and how they are using it. Statistics software takes the logs and puts the data into a more readable format.

You can learn this kind of information from your statistics:

- Referrals: The referrals tell you where visitors were before they came to your site. With this information, you can evaluate the effectiveness of your site promotional efforts, determine which search engines are referring visitors to you, and discover what other sites have included links to yours.

- Browser/Operating System: This statistic tells you the browsers that are being used to view your site and on what operating systems they run. You or your developer can use this information to optimize the site for the browsers that visit the most.

- Page Hits: The hits tell you which pages were visited the most and the least. This information helps you focus your design and development efforts on the pages that are the most important to your visitors.

- Visitors and Sessions: This information tells you which pages were visited and the length of time spent on each page. A Web browsing session begins the moment you open the first page of a site and ends when you leave the site. This statistic helps you determine how people are using your site. You can use this information to enhance or even revise your navigation. It also lets you know how many of the visits were real, versus how many were a single-page hit that lasted less than a minute. These quick hits are indicative of someone finding your site through a search engine, and then discovering your site did not have what they were looking for. Search engine spiders and email spambots also show up as quick hits as they search through your pages for keywords and email addresses.

You will find that a lot of organizations tout the number of hits they get on their site. That statistic can be very misleading, if not altogether meaningless. When you are trying to analyze what is really happening with your site, it is important to understand the difference between a page visit and a hit.

When you browse a Web page, the Web server logs a hit for that page. Then the server logs a hit for every element on that page that must be downloaded, such as each distinct image. It isn't unusual for a Web page to have ten or more images on it, so that page actually generates eleven hits in the log file: one for the page and ten for the images.

As you can see, just looking at the raw number of hits doesn't give you much useful information because every page can generate a different number of hits. What you really want to know is how many unique visitors you had and how many pages were actually viewed. Any decent Web statistics software can give you this information.

Like anything else relating to technology however, statistics software can range from a simple free "hit counter" to full-blown site analytics software that runs into the thousands of dollars. Unless you have massive ecommerce plans, the solution provided by your Web hosting company will probably give you all the basic information you need to know to make good decisions and improve your site over time.

Promotion Resources

Links to some of the many promotion resources available online.

General Web Marketing Info

- WilsonWeb - http://www.wilsonweb.com/

- Marketing Sherpa Free newsletters - http://www.marketingsherpa.com

- Web Site Tips - http://websitetips.com

- Virtual Promote (formerly Jim Tools) - http://www.virtualpromote.com

Big Search Engines and Directories

- Open Directory Project - http://www.dmoz.org

- Yahoo - http://www.yahoo.com

- Google - http://www.google.com

- AltaVista - http://www.altavista.com

- MSN - http://search.msn.com

Search Engine Optimization

- What Search Engine Spiders See - http://www.dlperry.com/what_search_engine_spiders_see.html

- Poodle Predictor See Your Site Like Google Does - http://www.gritechnologies.com/tools/spider.go?

- Search Engine Watch - http://searchenginewatch.com

- Web Pro World Forums - http://www.webproworld.com

- Web Position SEO Software - http://www.webposition.com

- Trellian SEO Tools - http://www.trellian.com/products.htm

Affiliate Programs and Information

- Ken Evoy's Affiliate Masters Course - http://www.sitesell.com

- Allan Gardyne's Associate Programs site and newsletter - http://www.associateprograms.com

- Commission Junction - http://www.cj.com

- LinkShare - http://www.linkshare.com

Ezine List Services and Autoresponders:

- Lyris - http://www.lyris.com/

- Constant Contact - http://www.constantcontact.com

- Topica - http://www.topica.com

- ProAutoResponder - http://www.proautoresponder.com/

- AWeber - http://www.aweber.com

- Get Response - http://www.getresponse.com

Email Marketing and Spam

- Email Universe - http://emailuniverse.com

- ClickZ - http://www.clickz.com

- Directory of Email Newsletters - http://new-list.com

- Email Sender and Provider Coalition - http://www.espcoalition.org

- SpamArrest Spam Filtering - http://www.spamarrest.com

PR Sites

- PR Web - http://www.prweb.com
- Businesswire - http://www.businesswire.com
- PR Newswire - http://www.prnewswire.com

Article Marketing

- Ezine Articles - http://www.ezinearticles.com
- Article Marketer Submission Service - http://www.articlemarketer.com

Blog Software

- Blogger - http://www.blogger.com
- Movable Type - http://www.movabletype.org
- WordPress - http://www.wordpress.com

Blog Aggregators

- Blogarama - http://www.blogarama.com/
- BlogUniverse - http://www.bloguniverse.com
- Globe Of Blogs - http://www.globeofblogs.com
- Technorati - http://www.technorati.com/

Ad Networks:

- Google AdSense - https://www.google.com/adsense/
- Kanoodle - http://www.kanoodle.com
- Yahoo Publisher Network - http://publisher.yahoo.com/
- ValueClick Media - http://www.valueclickmedia.com/

PayPerClick

- Google AdWords - https://adwords.google.com
- AdWords Keyword tool - https://adwords.google.com/select/KeywordToolExternal
- Yahoo Search Marketing - http://searchmarketing.yahoo.com
- Yahoo Keyword tool - http://searchmarketing.yahoo.com/rc/srch/
- WordTracker Keyword Research tool - http://www.wordtracker.com

Creating an Ecommerce Site

Business Basics

Once you have a Web site, at some point, you probably will add ecommerce. Even if your business is largely a service operation, you may want to sell a report that demonstrates your expertise. To understand the pros and cons of various ecommerce solutions, you must first understand how they work.

In general, the more control you have over a technology, the more expensive it is to implement. So before we jump into the details, let's discuss the business strategies behind implementing ecommerce solutions in the first place.

Before you invest heavily in ecommerce, get "proof of concept." We recommend that you start small, and if things work, expand incrementally. For example, often retail operations don't actually do very well on the Web, especially when you compare their Web sales to the cost of operating and maintaining the site. So if you are a retailer and you want to sell your products online, begin with a simple and inexpensive solution to verify that your customers are interested in purchasing through the Internet.

Once you have proof of concept (i.e., that customers actually want to buy certain items online), build an ecommerce site that gives them a chance to purchase those items. Then if you are going to do it, do it right. It is better to do a great job of the 80-percent solution than to do a poor job of the 100-percent solution. You can't get reliable proof of concept if your implementation is so bad that customers don't like to use it.

Usability is, and always will be, the key. Never forget that a Web site can help almost any business with one of its most costly aspects: customer service. If the site helps your customers do business with you, your Web site can do wonders for your bottom line.

Web-based software can automate many of the tedious, time-consuming, and expensive elements of your customer interface. The Internet allows even the smallest businesses to make information available to prospects 24/7. Product information and FAQs are there to help your customers make purchasing decisions, even if they decide to research your product at 2:00 in the morning.

Like most business decisions, ecommerce planning is paramount. Make your choices carefully and deliberately. If you need help making those decisions, find someone with experience and integrity and pay them to help you sort through your options. Just be aware that the recommendations you receive will probably be biased toward your advisor's most favored (or most profitable) solutions.

What is Ecommerce?

The subject of electronic commerce, or ecommerce, is full of hype and confusion. Ask ten people what ecommerce means, and you get ten different answers, even among knowledgeable people. After all, the Internet is a general-purpose medium for transferring information between two entities. The possibilities for its use are limitless.

Different businesses naturally take different approaches to doing business on the Internet. You may use the Internet as a marketing medium only. You may offer a catalog of products or services for online purchase. Your Web site may be hooked into your internal information system. You may conduct business with other companies through electronic transactions.

This section explores a few of the most common ecommerce options available to you. You will learn about options that are inexpensive to implement and some that require more of an investment. You will also learn how to start simply and add features as you can justify the expense.

Even though ecommerce means different things to different people, there is a common theme: using the Internet to transact business with your customers. Our focus in this book is on business, so we won't get into really high-end technologies that cost millions to implement. Instead, we concentrate on technologies that are easily accessible to organizations that don't have a full time IT staff. The topics we cover include Web storefronts, online payment and ASP (Application Service Provider) solutions.

The most important factor for any ecommerce enterprise is this: your Web site must justify its cost. Granted, you can't know for sure how much money your Web site will earn or save you. So that's why you start with the basics.

First, you must monitor your Web site's success as soon as you launch it. You must know when it starts to make significant revenue. Let your site pay for its own upgrades when possible. Of course, there are some intangibles: not everything your site does for you can be easily attached to an increase in revenue or a decrease in expenses. A Web site is like any other marketing strategy. You must do as much as possible to measure its success.

Your competition may influence your ecommerce decisions. You may need to create an ecommerce site simply to remain in the game. Even if you don't pay much attention to what the competition is up to, you can bet your customers do.

For example, nearly every bank in the country must now offer online banking to remain competitive. Yes, the investment required for a banking Web site is astronomical and the business benefit is difficult to measure. But the alternative is to lose customers or appear archaic.

Your goal, and one measure of your Web site's success, is market share. If in fact your business does require a major ecommerce investment to keep up with your competitors, turn this to your advantage. Study the sites of your rivals carefully. Note every aspect that seems slow, cumbersome, or confusing. Then do it better on your own site. Even a small improvement over your competition's sites can give you an edge!

Web Storefronts

When most people hear the term ecommerce they think of a Web storefront. The most obvious way to justify your investment in a business Web site is to use it to sell products and services, so creating a Web store seems obvious.

However, many companies have discovered that not everything sells well on the Web. It's true that almost any business can use a Web site to supplement its revenues and offer customer conveniences. Generating significant sales requires aggressive marketing through traditional and non-traditional channels.

We recommend that you scale your storefront based on the value you think it will bring to your company. Web storefronts consist of three distinct elements: catalog, order, and payment. Most high-end storefront solutions tightly integrate these elements. But for now, we'll look at them separately so you can understand each one and consider lower-cost alternatives.

The Catalog Element

The catalog element displays information about your products and services. Just like a hard copy catalog you get in the mail, it should provide enough information for your customers to make an informed buying decision (with product descriptions, prices, and photographs).

You can build an online catalog in two ways:

- Individually designed Web pages, called static pages. In the short term, most people opt for this option. You simply insert all your product information, including photos, into a Web page, which you build and code by hand.

- Pages generated from a database by Web software. This option is more expensive initially, but if you have a large number of products or your product information changes frequently, investing in software saves you money in the long run.

The Order Element

The order element keeps track of your customers' catalog selections. A low-end solution is a simple Buy Now button that takes the customer straight to a payment page. That approach works fine if you sell just one product.

You can see an example of a straightforward, single item order element on eBay. Many eBay sellers will give their customers the option of bypassing the bidding process. Instead, they display a flat price with a Buy It Now link.

Click that link, and you're taken to an order form where you can complete your purchase for that single item. This type of single order element makes a lot of sense on eBay. At an auction site, you expect to view thousands of individual items offered by thousands of individual sellers. You also expect to pay for each item separately.

It's easy to see how a single item order element would be extremely cumbersome for a site that offers multiple products. If you plan to sell more than a few products on your Web site, you'll need a shopping cart system.

Remember, you must never break the cardinal rule of ecommerce Web site design. Always make it easy for your customers to BUY. If you sell multiple products on your site, you'll naturally want your customers to be able to purchase multiple items with a single transaction. You'll also want your Web site to adjust shipping charges and taxes for your customer's convenience, based on the total order.

To make it easy for your customers to purchase multiple products, you need shopping cart software. This software remembers your customer's item selections, and calculates shipping and order totals automatically.

In fact, shopping cart software can make life easier for you, even when you have a relatively small number of products. If you have to update product information frequently, it's much easier to make these changes using shopping cart software because you can just change a couple of values that are stored in a database.

Selecting shopping cart software is not a simple task. You've got to ask yourself the right questions, and think through your customers' needs, before you design or purchase shopping cart software. (We'll cover shopping cart selection in great detail.)

The Payment Element

The payment element lets your customers pay for their orders. A low-end, low-tech solution is to just have your customer call you. This approach is far from ideal. Unless you've got a 24/7 customer service hotline, your customers will only be able to place orders during your regular business hours. Limited hours can turn off those customers located in time zones outside yours.

The reality is that most people who shop online actually want to make their purchase on your Web site. If you don't offer online payment, you're bound to lose customers. A low-end, low-cost option would be to use a third-party payment processor like PayPal or CCNow.

These low-end, low-tech third-party services have their advantages. Your initial cost is low, and integration into your site does not require anything more than basic HTML skills. Plus if you do not have your own merchant account, which lets you accept credit card payments, you can skip the trouble and expense of obtaining one. If you are on a limited budget and selling only a few products, these low-end options can be a good way to accept payments on a proof-of-concept Web site.

Low-tech third-party services have disadvantages as well. If you sell a lot of different products on your site, or if your monthly sales are substantial, you may end up paying more in the long run. Third-party payment processors generally charge a percentage of each transaction. Over time, these transactions may add up and be more expensive than owning your own shopping cart software and using your own merchant account. You also may not have a lot of control over the payment interface your customer sees.

A high-end solution is to use Web software that accepts credit card information directly from your site. This software authorizes payment through an Internet payment gateway service. If you already have a merchant account for your business, this solution gives you more control over exactly how your payment interface will look. (We'll talk about payment gateways in a later section.)

Storefront Options

The many possible configurations for a Web-based storefront can get confusing quickly! To simplify matters, let's concentrate on your answers to the following questions.

1. Do you require a shopping cart?

2. How much control do you need over the appearance of the storefront?

3. Do you want to accept credit card payments over the Internet?

Really think about the answers to these questions. They have a direct impact on how expensive your storefront will be! Make sure you give your Web developer the answers to these questions up front. Then he or she can build the most cost-effective solutions into your Web site from the beginning.

After all, there is no sense paying for a full-featured shopping cart if you just plan to sell a single product and you want customers to phone their orders in to you!

How Do You Decide?

You own a business for many reasons. Maybe you want to be your own boss. Or you want to do what you love or add excitement to your life. Most importantly, you're in business to make a profit. So it's only logical that the best ecommerce solution for your business has to be profitable.

Before you decide on any solution, you should realistically estimate the value of a Web storefront and budget accordingly. You may need a combination of alternatives to get the best return on investment (ROI).

If your Web site is going to require some type of shopping cart software, first you'll probably talk to your Web developer about it. He or she may have a strong preference for one shopping cart system over another.

That recommendation may be great in your situation. Or it might not. In the rest of this section, we explain how you can determine which of the many, many options out there is really the right one for you.

The ASP Question

An Application Service Provider (or ASP) gives you access to specialized software that runs on their server over the Internet. ASPs can include storefront services. Sometimes they are also referred to as a "hosted application." In other words, the software is running on someone else's Web site, not yours.

You or your employees can use a browser to navigate to the service provider's Web site. At the site, they log into the service. They can update your storefront by adding new products or changing prices.

The ASP software runs on the service provider's server. Your product data is stored in a database on the service provider's network. Instead of buying or creating your own software, you pay an access fee for using their software. The fees vary according to the type of service you need and the length of contract.

ASPs can host your entire site or just a part of it, such as the shopping cart. You can also simply choose to link to the storefront service from a site hosted elsewhere. Either way, this solution is often the least expensive way to get started. The only downside is that you have a lot less control over the appearance and function of your storefront. You've probably bought items over the Internet yourself and noticed when you entered the checkout that suddenly the appearance of the site changes dramatically or the text on the Address bar shows a different URL.

As with any software licensing arrangement, there are advantages and disadvantages to using an ASP. The primary advantage is that the software vendor is responsible for maintaining the service. All you have to do is pay a monthly fee for it and use it. The ASP makes sure the service is available. The ASP is responsible for implementing software upgrades. Your day-to-day technology burden is considerably lighter this way. Just make sure you review your Service License Agreement (SLA), so you know who is responsible for certain important functions like backups.

The primary disadvantage of using an ASP is your lack of control. You are 100% dependent upon the ASP to live up to the performance standards spelled out in the SLA. Also, since an ASP is a Web service, the quality of their Internet connection is of critical importance. If you (or your customers) can't get connected, nobody can use the service!

You also have little control if the software has a bug that affects you. If you are working with an ASP and you are the only user affected, expect a slow turnaround for the repair. If your ASP goes out of business, you either have to find someone else who offers the same software, or start over with new software. After all the work of setting up the site and ordering products this scenario is not appealing.

With all these disadvantages, why do so many businesses opt for outsourced solutions like ASP applications? Because they can save big money. In spite of the limitations of ASPs, the cost savings often outweigh the risks by a large margin.

With an ASP, the total cost of your storefront is much lower. You don't have to pay to license software and you don't need to hire someone to build or maintain your site. You can leave almost all of the technical details to the technicians at the ASP. You just concentrate on making and selling products.

Shopping Cart Software

If you decide against a hosted (ASP) solution, obviously you have other options. The company who hosts your Web site may offer shopping cart software that you can integrate with your Web site. This solution usually gives you more control over the appearance of your storefront than an ASP. It may also give you more payment processing alternatives.

However, with this solution you will need some professional help, at least at the beginning. Adding out-of-the-box software to your existing Web site, and tweaking it to look and work just right, may take many hours of Web development time. This integration project may not be something you want to try to do yourself.

If you host your own Web site on your own server, you can choose to purchase and install whatever storefront software you feel best suits your needs. This solution gives you the most flexibility and control. Unfortunately, it generally costs much more than the other two alternatives.

However, investing in your own software and server may allow you to save money over the long haul because you don't have monthly fees. You also may be able to connect your storefront with your other information systems, such as your accounting program. This connection may add a layer of complexity to your technology though. Whenever a system gets more complex, it gets more expensive. If nothing else, you will need to hire more expert help to tune and maintain these systems, and to fix them when something goes awry.

Shopping cart software consists of two distinct elements:

- An administration site. You use this interface to manage your product catalog and to process received orders.

- A public site. This part is what your customers see. They use it to select the products they want and to pay for their order.

Both elements share a database. This area is where you store the product catalog and order information in the database. All your updates and changes go into this database as well.

When you go hunting for a shopping cart, you are confronted with a daunting selection of products. They have wildly different prices, features, and configurations.

Before you can make an informed decision, you must figure out which product matches your requirements. Of course, that means you must understand your requirements. So if you haven't yet developed Web site goals, a Web site plan, and a bubble diagram, go back and do this now.

Investing in shopping cart software before you've done your basic site architecture always leads to expensive mistakes! Before you start shopping for a shopping cart, you must take your Web site hosting arrangements into account. Your host may already offer a shopping cart, with at least some support, as part of your hosting plan.

If you decide you want a third-party shopping cart, you'll have to install software on the host's computer. Installing software is always a bit risky for your host! So investigate the shopping cart options offered by your host before you go further. If it will work for you, choosing your host's shopping cart might save you considerable money and hassle down the line. If you go for the ASP option, you have to integrate it with your main site. Integration involves linking to the third-party service.

When evaluating shopping cart software, many people focus on just the public component because that is what the customer sees. However, don't forget to assess whether or not you can stand to use the administration interface!

A poorly designed administration site that is slow or cumbersome is a maintenance nightmare. Remember, the shopping cart should make your life easier, too!

Shopping Cart Features

Not all shopping carts work the same. Don't lay down money for shopping cart software until you verify that the software can do what you want. This statement seems obvious, but most people assume all shopping carts must have the features they need. After all, doesn't everyone else need those same features? In a word: No. Most shopping cart companies also have links to sites that use their software. Go and try it out on a real, functional site. If you hate using it, your customers will too.

Think very carefully about the following features when considering shopping cart software alternatives:

- Categories/Subcategories: If you have a large product line, you need a way to organize those products into categories, and possibly even subcategories. For example, suppose you run a huge plant farm and nursery. You might offer various pine seedlings in the Conifer subcategory, which would be under the Trees category. Your shopping cart software should let you update and move product information between categories and subcategories easily.

- Product Listing and Detail: Visitors should be able to view a list of products in a particular subcategory, along with a small photo and short description. When visitors click a single product, you should be able to show them a bigger photo and complete description. This feature lets visitors control their shopping experience. They can browse quickly through your catalog, and wait for a larger photo to download on only the products they select.

- Shipping: Some shopping carts let you control shipping by the weight of the order. Some allow you to choose different criteria for calculating shipping, such as basing it on the price of the order. If you need to add handling or rush fees, make sure you have this option. Shipping invariably ends up being far more problematic than people realize, so look into this question VERY carefully before you select a cart.

- Taxes: Some shopping carts allow only one regional tax. Others allow for multiple taxation options. If you need to control tax on an item-by-item basis, make sure the cart has this capability.

- Price Levels: Most shopping carts allow only a single price level. Others allow "membership" pricing, which can create powerful incentives for repeat business. Customers can join as members, then log in with a membership ID or enter a code at checkout for special pricing.

- Coupons: This feature lets you set up coupon codes that your customers can use at checkout to receive a discount on a particular product or on the order as a whole. Coupons can be important if you are trying to generate new or repeat business.

- Product Options: With this feature you can specify product options. For example, you could allow customers to select a color for a shirt. You can even configure these options to affect the price of the product. For example, solid colors are $10.99; stripes are $11.99.

- Payment Gateway Support: Not all shopping carts work with all payment gateways (also called payment processors). If you already have an Internet payment gateway, make sure the shopping cart supports it! (We talk more about payment processors in the upcoming *Why the Payment Gateway is Important* section.) Selecting a cart that doesn't support the payment gateway you need is a problem because you have a cart that can't accept payment from your customers.

- Customization: Some shopping carts let you design and upload templates that control the display of your product catalog. Others are more limited; they may only let you add a logo or choose a color scheme. Having complete design flexibility means your shopping cart will integrate seamlessly with the look and feel of the rest of your Web site for a more professional impression. It's also more work to set up, so you must decide whether this design integration is worth the extra investment.

This list is not exhaustive. It's designed to get you thinking seriously about how you want your customer's shopping experience to work. As you think about these features, make a list of everything you want your shopping cart to do. Go over this list with your Web developer, so you can choose the solution that offers the features and options that are most important to you.

Understanding Online Payment

These days, a mind-boggling array of shopping cart options exists. But it wasn't always the case. A few years ago, James wrote a custom Web shopping cart software for one of our customers. The most difficult part of the project was accepting credit card payments from customers online.

The difficulty wasn't so much in the coding of the software interface (although that had its challenges). The biggest problem was understanding how Internet payments are processed in general.

Even with all of James' experience in programming and development, he was surprised at the complexity of the issue. We realized that we weren't the only ones who were confused. Our clients aren't exactly systems engineers; they are running a business. Because of their ignorance, they could have purchased the wrong solution several times over before finally getting it right.

We have come to realize that online payment is probably the most misunderstood element of an ecommerce Web site. It's a complex topic. The ecommerce newbie can get suckered into paying for too much, too little, or the wrong things.

The only way to correct the situation is to arm yourself with knowledge. You can save yourself a lot of headaches and expense if you understand the basics. So unlike many books or articles that just say, "go use this shopping cart," we're going to explain the process, so you actually understand what's going on.

Accepting Credit Cards

The best way to understand Internet payment processing is to compare it to a traditional point-of-sale scenario. The goal of any payment system is to transfer money from the customer's credit card account to your merchant account. The first step in accepting credit card payments of any kind is to establish a merchant account.

What is a Merchant Account?

A merchant account is a special account you set up with your bank for receiving credit card payments. Your merchant account is where all your payments are deposited. Customer credits and merchant account fees are also withdrawn from this account. The financial institution that sets up your merchant account is called the acquiring institution, because it acquires the credit card payments.

If your bank offers Internet merchant services, they may let you use your existing business bank account as your merchant account. If you need a new account, be prepared to give the financial institution a couple of weeks to set it up.

You may already have a merchant account for accepting credit cards over the phone or at your bricks-and-mortar business. However, your current merchant account may not allow Internet transactions. There are two types of merchant accounts: Card Present and Card Not Present accounts.

- Card Present accounts are usually associated with a point-of-sale card swipe terminal. The customer makes a face-to-face purchase by handing you a physical credit card.

- Card Not Present accounts are also called MOTO accounts (Mail Order/ Telephone Order). These are for situations where the customer is not present at the point of sale.

All Internet transactions are treated as Card Not Present transactions. Because Card Not Present accounts are more risky, the fee structures are different. Even if you already have a Card Present type merchant account for your bricks-and-mortar store, you may have to get a new merchant account for your Web store.

The bottom line is before you even think about taking payments online, make sure you've got a merchant account that actually works for Internet transactions. As we said, setting this up may take time, so start the process as soon as possible.

Understanding How Credit Card Payments Work

A credit card transaction is usually completed in three steps: authorization, capture, and settlement.

- Authorization verifies that the customer's card is good for the transaction.

- Capture collects the transactions you are ready to settle into a batch.

- Settlement transfers the money from your customer's credit card account to your merchant account.

In a point-of-sale scenario, the customer comes to your store and hands you a card. You then run the card through a card swipe terminal, or enter the credit card numbers into personal computer software.

The terminal or software connects with the banking network and performs authorization. Later that day, the software will capture the transactions and submit the batch. After the batch gets processed, settlement occurs and money is deposited in your merchant account.

Why the Payment Gateway is Important

In an Internet payment scenario, there's no face-to-face encounter as there is in a store. Instead, you use a payment gateway to perform authorization, capture, and settlement. A payment gateway is also called an Internet payment processor. Examples of payment gateways are VeriSign and Authorize.net.

The payment gateway is vital because it gives your Web site the power to collect credit card information and authorization without human intervention. Instead of handing you a credit card, the customer chooses items from your Web site and collects them in your ecommerce shopping cart.

The payment gateway then:

- Receives payment requests from the shopping cart software.

- Connects to the banking network to authorize the requests.

- Returns the authorization (or decline) code to the shopping cart for disposition.

- Keeps a record of the transaction.

At the end of the day, you log in to the payment processor's merchant interface to:

- Capture the transactions for orders you shipped, or to enter credits and voids. (You can usually configure the gateway or the shopping cart to capture automatically for you.)

Finally, once per day, the gateway connects to the banking network and performs settlement of the captured transaction batch.

Here is where some of the confusion surrounding online payment systems really begins: the payment gateway is usually a separate service that you must sign up for. It has its own setup fees, per-transaction fees, and minimum monthly charges.

The entity that arranged your merchant account is called your acquiring financial institution. It might be your bank, or it might be an external merchant account service. It is always simplest if you just ask the acquiring financial institution for a payment gateway recommendation.

Getting this recommendation is important because not all payment gateways work with all banking networks. They are like automobile parts. A connector from one component won't necessarily fit another component. Never assume that various pieces of your payment system are built from standard parts.

It also makes good **economic** sense to ask your acquiring institution for a recommendation. You might get a discount on the payment gateway service charges if you order their recommended gateway. Finally, as if all this weren't complicated enough, not all payment gateways work with all shopping carts. So before you choose a gateway, make sure that your shopping cart supports it. Otherwise you'll have to select a shopping cart that supports your gateway.

The payment gateway connects your Web site with your merchant account's banking network. It's how you get paid for orders. So it must be compatible with everything. Most payment gateways offer similar services for a similar price. You should read the fine print carefully, and do some comparison-shopping. Pricing is ultimately dependent on how much Web business you plan to transact. For example, if you expect many small transactions, then the setup and monthly fees are not as significant as the per-transaction fees.

How Internet Payments Work

Nothing is more important in business than getting paid. So how exactly does the money get from the customer's credit card account to your merchant account? Here is a diagram you can refer to as you read this section.

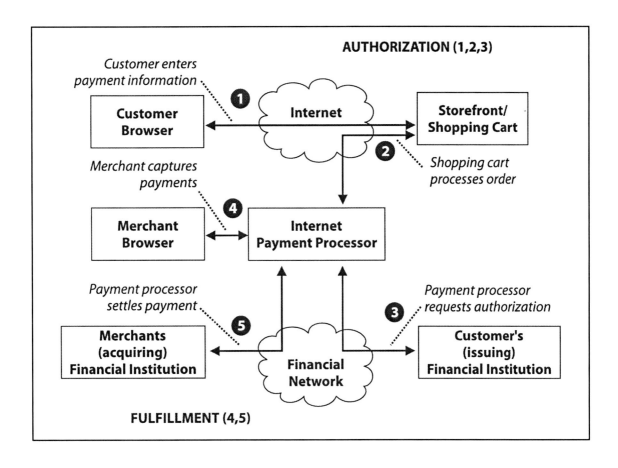

The Internet purchase process is broken up into two distinct phases: authorization and fulfillment.

Steps 1, 2, and 3 represent the authorization phase, and are indicated with dotted lines. Authorization verifies that the customer has the necessary funds available at the time the sale is made.

Steps 4 and 5 represent fulfillment, shown with solid lines. Fulfillment says that you have shipped the order, so the funds are now rightfully yours.

Now let's follow your money step-by-step:

1. The customer enters credit card information on your Web site and submits an order.

2. The shopping cart software processes the order. It sends information about the customer, and the dollar amount of the charge to the payment gateway.

3. The payment gateway requests authorization from the customer's financial institution through the banking network. It electronically negotiates with the banking network to get an authorization (or failure) code. The authorization phase is now complete.

4. The merchant uses administration tools provided by either the shopping cart or the payment gateway to capture payments for orders that have been shipped.

5. The payment gateway settles captured payments, usually on a nightly basis. Funds actually transfer from the customer's financial institution to your financial institution at this point. This step completes the fulfillment phase.

Depending upon what you sell and how you fill orders, there may or may not be a time lapse between the authorization and fulfillment. For example, you may sell software or other digital products that the customer receives immediately, either via email or through download, as soon as the order is confirmed. This type of fulfillment is called a payload. With a payload, you can capture payments immediately.

Also, if you regularly process orders on a daily basis, your payment processor may let you automatically mark your transactions for capture at the end of each day. This process is called Auto-Capture. It saves you time, since you don't have to manually execute step 4.

Merchant Interface

After you start receiving orders through your Web site, you need a way to capture, void, and refund charges. Your payment gateway should give you a browser-based merchant interface for this purpose. A merchant interface is just a fancy name for the Web page you use to look at all your transactions online and make any manual changes.

You go to a Web page on the payment gateway's Web site to monitor your transactions. Once you log in, you can review your current transactions and your transaction history. Some services even let you download your transaction history so you can import it into your accounting program or other software.

Some merchant interfaces require you to log in at the end of each day so you can capture payments. You mark the payments for shipped orders. That night, the payment gateway settles the payments, and transfers the funds from the customer's financial institution (called the issuing financial institution) to your financial institution (called the acquiring financial institution). You might also use the merchant interface to process refunds when customers return items to you.

Potential Payment Trouble Spots

You may be thinking that this doesn't sound so complicated after all. You're right. Theoretically, the process is simple! It's the logistics of implementing this process that cause all the trouble and can cost you. So let's go through all the things that can go wrong. After all, forewarned is forearmed. If you know where all the potentially costly pitfalls are, you will be less vulnerable as you build your first ecommerce site.

Potential Trouble Spot #1: Your Customer and Your Shopping Cart Don't Get Along.

For example, your customer may want to use American Express or Discover, but your merchant account may only accept Visa and MasterCard. Solving this problem is relatively simple. Clearly state up front the cards you accept!

It's surprising how many Web sites fail to tell their customers which cards they accept. It isn't a problem with technology. It's a communication issue. Ideally you should set up your account to accept Visa, MasterCard, American Express, and Discover. Unfortunately, American Express and Discover require their own separate arrangements with your merchant service. You may decide it is not worth the extra trouble or expense.

A more serious problem occurs when your shopping cart software isn't designed for optimum usability. Customers may not like using it. For example, the interface may be difficult to understand. Spend some time testing the software. If you hate using it, your customers probably will too.

Potential Trouble Spot #2: Your Shopping Cart Software Won't Work With Your Payment Gateway.

Not all shopping carts support all payment gateways. For example, your shopping cart may support Authorize.net, but not VeriSign.

How is this possible? Even though your shopping cart software has order processing features, it may or may not be able to communicate with the payment gateway's merchant interface. Each payment gateway has its own rules for how transactions must be formatted.

Potential Trouble Spot #3: Your Merchant Account Doesn't Accept Online Payments.

As we mentioned, not all merchant accounts can be used to accept Internet payments. Internet transactions are considered more risky than traditional point-of-sale transactions, so financial institutions use different fee schedules to accommodate that risk.

Potential Trouble Spot #4: Your Payment Gateway Won't Work With Your Merchant Account.

Asking one simple question at the very beginning can save you from this hassle. Always ask whether your payment gateway can communicate with your financial institution's banking network. If it can't, there is simply no way for the payment gateway to settle payments into your merchant account. In other words, you won't get paid!

Small Budget Payment Alternatives

The setup charges and monthly fees associated with a merchant account may be too steep for many small businesses. Minimum monthly charges for merchant accounts can be substantial, and may not be cost effective until you start to make a certain amount of sales. The good news is there are alternatives to merchant accounts that can save you some money.

The simplest way to save money on Internet payment systems is not to do it! You can ask customers to come to your store, call in their order over the telephone, or print an order sheet and mail it. The problem is that all this manual labor can add up to far more than the monthly cost of a merchant account! Online payment processing lets you make sales with no human intervention. It saves on labor costs and telephone charges and lowers the chance of human error in the order taking process.

Plus, the whole point of your Web site is to make it easier for your customers to do business with you. Your customers have become accustomed to the convenience of 24/7 online ordering because computers don't need sleep. Internet shoppers participate in a tacit "Web culture." Part of that culture demands an Internet-based ordering solution.

Fortunately, solutions exist that fall between no Internet payment processing and a fully automated solution with a dedicated merchant account. An increasing number of services provide simplified merchant accounts. Usually they are hosted shopping cart solutions that include merchant account and payment processing for a monthly fee.

With this type of integrated service, you don't have to worry about compatibility issues between your payment gateway, shopping cart, and merchant account. So why would you sign up for your own Internet merchant account when you can use one of these less expensive alternatives? The answer is control.

In getting your own merchant account, you have more control over which shopping cart you can use. You also control where your product and customer data is hosted. Accessing this information directly can make a big difference when your business grows larger.

The PayPal Alternative

When you're just starting out testing the waters, dealing with a merchant account, shopping cart and so forth may be more of an expenditure than you are willing (or able) to undertake. Even the monthly fees for a bundled solution might be a stretch. Another alternative is to just use PayPal.

PayPal (http://www.paypal.com/) is currently the most popular third-party Internet payment processor. Anyone who makes purchases on eBay is probably familiar with PayPal.

Here's the way it works:

- PayPal establishes an account for you.

- When customers place an order on your Web site, your site sends them to the PayPal site for payment through a special link. This PayPal link includes a code that identifies your company.

- When the customer pays, PayPal deducts a service charge and deposits the payment into your PayPal account.

- You periodically request payment from PayPal via check or direct deposit to your bank account.

The advantage of PayPal is that it is free of setup fees and monthly service charges. You pay a reasonable per-transaction charge and that is it. It used to be that customers had to sign up with PayPal to buy from you, but that is no longer the case. And for customers who are already PayPal users, the payment procedure is extremely simple because they can draw money right out of their PayPal account. Customers without an account can either go through the free registration process or just use a credit card to complete the purchase.

PayPal has its limitations. Although you no longer have to be a PayPal user to buy, it's easier if you are. And because the interface forces you to go to a separate site it can turn potential customers off. Some people become confused or lost when they go to the PayPal site, which includes an email message exchange with PayPal. It also doesn't look professional. Many amateurish business sites use PayPal and a tremendous amount of spoofed "phishing" email scams appear to have a return PayPal email address (even though they actually aren't from PayPal).

PayPal IPN

Unless you use a shopping cart that was specifically designed to support PayPal, delivering electronic payload (products like ebooks for example) can be risky. The simple approach is to set up a download page and let PayPal send customers who complete the payment process to that page. However, it is easy for even casual hackers to fake the download page URL and retrieve your offering without paying for it.

Fortunately, PayPal offers a solution to this problem: Instant Payment Notification (IPN). Implemented correctly, IPN is a secure way to guarantee that customers paid for your product before they received access to a download. To use IPN, your shopping cart or other ecommerce software must have a gateway page specifically designed to accept IPN transactions. You configure your PayPal account to send payment notifications to the URL of that gateway page. When customers make a purchase on your site, PayPal sends the details of the transaction to the configured URL. The gateway page processes the transaction and performs whatever action is necessary to release the product to the customer.

Setting up IPN support on your Web site is, as they say, a non-trivial exercise. If you want to use PayPal as your payment processor for any kind of electronic download, be sure to find ecommerce software that supports IPN.

Although it isn't perfect, PayPal is a good low-budget way to experiment with adding ecommerce features to your Web site. With millions of current users and more signing up every day, there must be something right about it.

Payment Security

Everyone is concerned with security these days, and for good reason. The Internet is a global network of computers with a large community of hackers. Hackers are nothing more than electronic vandals and/or thieves.

These folks have tools that allow them to intercept and review information sent across the Internet. Because of these hacker ploys, you should never send critical passwords or any other confidential information using normal email. Online protection for yourself, and your customers, is as important as offline security.

SSL and Digital Certificates

It may come as a shock, but the Web forms you use to enter your credit card information are no more secure than email, unless you take precautions to make them so. That lack of security is why Secured Sockets Layer (SSL) exists.

To apply SSL to a Web site, you must acquire a digital certificate from a qualified certificate authority, such as VeriSign or Thawte. The digital certificate associates a specific domain (like http://shop.logicalexpressions.com/) with a key that uniquely identifies it. Your Web host installs the certificate on the server that hosts your domain.

When visitors navigate to a secure page on your site, they can use their browser to verify your identity through the certificate. In Internet Explorer, you can right-click on the secure page, select Properties, and click the Certificates button.

The certificate does more than just establish your identity. It also lets you encrypt all communications between the browser and the server. Encrypting your communications makes it nearly impossible (and totally impractical) to decipher the contents of a message. It means your customers can enter sensitive information into a form, and feel confident that it really is secure!

Currently, two common levels of encryption are available:

- 40-bit encryption. Shopping sites typically use 40-bit encryption, which is supported by most browsers.

- 128-bit encryption. Your bank probably requires 128-bit encryption for you to use its online banking functions. Although 128-bit encryption is more secure (the more bits, the more difficult it is to decode a message), it is not supported by older browsers. Also the certificate is more expensive.

You may not need a digital certificate if your shopping cart host provides a common checkout facility for all vendors. In that case, the host has the certificate, and lets you borrow it to process secure transactions.

The downside of this approach is that your secured pages must run under the host's domain name. This situation may confuse your customers and make it difficult for them to navigate your site.

So you think you need your own digital certificate? Then expect to pay from $50 to $350 per year, depending upon who you buy it from and whether you get a multiple-year or renewal discount.

Understand Customer Concerns

In these days of major hacker attacks and endless spam, you should deal up front with customer concerns about security and privacy. Make your visitors feel comfortable as quickly and easily as possible by addressing the following issues right on your site:

How secure is my credit card information?

Handle this concern with an easily accessible security link that explains why your site is secure. Explain the techniques you use such as SSL encryption. To increase your credibility, also display the logo of the authority that issued your digital certificate.

Before you turn your site live, be very sure your shopping cart's payment page goes into secure mode before you prompt for a credit card number. Some sites don't switch to secure mode until they actually send the form. Although this process works fine, visitors don't have the assurance of that little lock displaying in their browser window.

As for storing credit card numbers, we recommend that you just don't do it. Once your shopping cart passes the transaction on to the payment gateway, you really don't need to retain the credit card number. Storing it is a source of potential liability for you. (Hackers think of stored credit card numbers as bait!)

If you have the option, have your shopping cart mask out the number or discard it entirely. Customers will have to enter their credit card number every time they make a purchase. But it's reassuring to know that the site isn't storing numbers on file somewhere.

What do you do with my personal information?

Next to your security policy, your customer will most want to know where you stand on privacy. If you value your customers, don't share their private information with other organizations. Likewise, never add their email address to your newsletter or other emarketing list without their permission.

As we've said, we are firm believers in the opt-in approach to electronic communications. It's better for your customers, and it's safer for you. When your customers opt-in, they explicitly do something to indicate they want email from you. They type in their email address and push a button. They take action that says they want to be included in your mailings.

Compare this policy with opt-out, where customers have to do something explicit to avoid receiving your email. You might think you are doing your customers a favor by sending them free information and the latest sale prices. Most people consider anything they didn't ask for to be junk, regardless of how marvelous the sender thinks it is.

How long will it take for my order to arrive?

Your customers want their order as quickly as possible. So your site should clearly state how long it takes for you to process and ship the order. Ideally, you should ship within 24 hours. It is particularly important to ship quickly if you let customers select rapid delivery options (like overnight), and if you charge their credit card right away.

What is happening to my order?

Let your customer know when you receive their order and when you have shipped their order. A simple email message will suffice. If several steps are required to process the order (as in custom merchandise), let your customers check the status of their order through your Web site.

Am I really getting a good deal here?

Customers understand that price is not the only consideration, even for commodity items. Make sure your site explains why buying from you is better than buying from your competition. Tout your commitment to only offering the highest quality merchandise. Or remind them of your excellent return policy, free shipping, or whatever else makes your products and service superior.

What if there is something wrong with my order?

One real disadvantage of buying online is that you can't examine your purchase before you buy it. You can't tell that the shirts run large or that the color in the photograph is not accurate.

Make your return policy very clear, and be as generous as possible. It is easy for customers to dispute a purchase. Disputes can result in an expensive charge-back to your merchant account. Besides, you want your customers to be happy so they will buy from you again.

If you succeed in making your customers feel comfortable buying from you, they usually won't bother to shop elsewhere. Most customers won't put themselves through tedious comparison-shopping over and over again.

Many times, they go through the process once, and then stick with a vendor. Make sure you come out on top during that selection process, and your odds are good for retaining that customer for a long time.

Ecommerce Resources

Links to a few of the larger shopping cart solutions and payment gateways.

Hosted Solutions:

- 1shoppingcart - http://www.1shoppingcart.com/

- PayPal - http://www.paypal.com

- ProStores - http://www.prostores.com/

- Yahoo Stores - http://smallbusiness.yahoo.com/ecommerce/

Shopping Cart Software:

- XCart PHP Shopping Cart - http://www.x-cart.com/

- Pinnacle Cart PHP shopping cart - http://www.pinnaclecart.com

- Miva Merchant - http://www.miva.com/us/

- VP ASP - http://www.vpasp.com

- We have used Ecommerce Templates for our shopping cart sites: http://www.ecommercetemplates.com/

Payment Gateways:

- Authorize.Net - http://www.authorize.net

- VeriSign - http://www.verisign.com

- 2CheckOut.com - http://www.2checkout.com/

- WorldPay.com - http://www.worldpay.com/usa/

Business Operations and Practices

Formulate a Strategy

Having read through this book, you are probably now painfully aware exactly how much work having a Web business is. You have to think about many things. Whether you perform these tasks yourself or outsource them, you still have to provide input and make decisions. You have to:

- Create content
- Select systems and software
- Find people to help you
- Work with customers

These tasks may involve:

- Copywriting
- Web design
- Programming
- Sales and marketing
- Research and analysis
- And much more

If you're feeling overwhelmed or frustrated, we encourage you to take a deep breath and focus on just one thing: planning. Do not try and do everything at once and don't chase every marketing opportunity in your quest to figure out what to do. You'll only end up spinning your wheels and getting burnt out.

As we've mentioned, we operate about 25 Web sites at this point. Many of them are quite large. We struggle with this level of overwhelm ourselves. When that happens, we know we need to sit down and "strategize."

Every business needs a strategy. As we said on the first pages of this book, you wouldn't go into pig farming without learning anything about pigs. Now you know something about Web business, so it's time to take that information and work out a plan that is right for you.

Start with a Web site. Just one. Either create the site yourself or select a Web developer following our guidelines. Now follow these steps. Think of this as your one-page plan to get your site online:

The Plan

1. Give the Web developer your current marketing materials that demonstrate your logo and company color scheme and site references that show your preferred design style.

2. Reserve your domain name.

3. When it's ready, review and approve site design.

4. Provide additional site copy and images for Web site if needed.

5. Select a hosting company following the recommendations in this book.

6. Using the domain registrar admin interface, set the DNS server names to use the host's DNS servers (get this info from the host). Allow 24 hours to propagate.

7. Set up domain email accounts or ask your hosting company to do it.

8. Get FTP login information from the host and give it to your Web developer.

9. Review and approve final site content and upload the files to your new site.

If or when you opt to move into ecommerce:

10. Get a merchant account and select a payment gateway.

11. Purchase an SSL certificate. (Note: This requires a certificate request file from the host.)

12. Configure the shopping cart to use the payment gateway.

13. Configure the cart to use your preferred shipping settings, such as weight or price-based shipping. Register with UPS or USPS if your shopping cart gets shipping information from these companies.

14. Enter images and product descriptions into the shopping cart product catalog.

Common Web Store Setup Costs

When you set up a Web storefront that is capable of accepting credit card payments, you have to plan for certain costs for setup and to process transactions. As we've explained throughout the book, some costs may be combined with others, depending on how you set up the site. For example, many merchant accounts bundle in costs for the payment gateway.

Typical Setup Costs

When you are setting your budget, these are the line items you may need. As of this writing, creating even a simple shopping cart site will probably cost you at least $2,000.

- **Merchant Account**: This is a special holding account for funds you receive or refund through your Internet payment gateway. It may be tied directly to your business bank account, or it may be a separate account entirely.

- **Payment Gateway**: Your web store submits transactions to your payment gateway for processing. The payment gateway gives you a browser-based interface that lets you enter, void, refund, and capture credit card transactions. It is the link between your Web site and your merchant account.

- **Security (SSL) Certificate**: Your Web site must have a security certificate assigned to it in order for it to securely process credit card transactions through a Web page. The certificate identifies who you are and encrypts the transaction data that is transmitted from your customer's browser to your Web site.

- **Hosting**: Your Web site must be placed on a Web server that is connected via a high-speed connection to the Internet. Whether you manage this machine yourself or outsource your site to a hosting company, you will have to pay to set up your Web site and all of the software that you want to run on your site.

- **Domain Name**: You should acquire a unique domain name that matches your business name. Use that domain name for all of your Internet business activities.

- **Shopping Cart Software**: A Web storefront is really a software program that is designed to run on a Web server. Depending upon your requirements, the software may be very expensive, or it might be very inexpensive.

- **Integration and Development**: Rarely will you find Web storefront software that behaves and looks the way you want. If you want to alter the design of the pages or add features, expect to pay a Web designer and/or developer to customize the storefront software for you. Additionally, you may need to pay someone to install and configure the software for you.

Recurring Costs

Along with hosting, you will need to account for these recurring costs.

- **Merchant Account**: Your merchant account has minimum monthly charges associated with it. When you go over a certain number of transactions, expect to pay additional per-transaction fees.

- **Payment Gateway**: Your payment gateway also has minimum monthly charges and per-transaction charges.

Operating an Internet Product Business

If you have never run a mail-order, telephone-order, or Internet-based product business before, you may be surprised at the amount of additional work involved.

When you operate a bricks-and-mortar storefront, you deal with inventory, stocking, and point-of-sale issues. With a Web storefront, you have all those issues and more.

Here are some points of pain when selling products over the Internet:

Capturing Payments

Although your Web site authorizes customer payments for you, you usually still have to capture those payments once a day through your payment gateway's merchant interface. However, you can only capture the payments associated with orders that you have shipped.

Order Accounting
Your shopping cart software may or may not support direct export to your accounting software. If it doesn't, be prepared to manually transfer your orders.

Discount Accounting
Even if your Web storefront supports exporting to your accounting software, there is a good possibility that it won't transfer all of the information you need to properly analyze your sales. For example, if you have different coupons for different types of discounts, you'll want to create reports that show how those discounts have affected your sales. If your shopping cart does not distinguish the source of a discount in the export file, then that important information will not transfer into your accounting software.

Shipping Charges
Even if your Web store has direct links to shipping charge calculation services like the USPS and UPS, managing shipping charges can be tricky, particularly if you ship large or irregularly shaped packages. The automated services can't help you account for your handling costs, and your shopping cart software probably does not give you a way to do that on an item-level basis either.

Customer Relationship Management
Although it depends a lot upon your shopping cart software and your accounting software, you probably don't have good tools for managing your customer relationships. For example, extracting information about your best customers and performing sales analysis can be a challenge. But those activities are important to providing superior customer service and giving your business an edge over your competition. You may find it necessary to invest in better or additional software to get the analytics and customer communication tools you need.

Packing and Shipping
It is easy to underestimate the amount of time it takes to properly prepare an order for shipping. You need to have the right packing materials for the object at hand, and

those materials can be expensive. You need a way to create labels easily. Even if it only takes five minutes per package, a mere twelve orders will take you an hour to prepare.

Inventory Management

Your Web storefront can probably track inventory for you, but you are still responsible for keeping the storefront in sync with your physical inventory. If you get a return, you need to add that item back into the shopping cart to sell it again. If someone places an order by phone, you need to remove the sold items from the available store inventory. If you receive a new shipment of items for resale, those items need to be added to your Web storefront as well.

Dealing with Miscreants

Once you have a site and particularly if you start to build a sense of community among your Web site's visitors, you'll have to deal with the miscreants in the crowd. Every community has them, and the Internet is no exception. These are the people who feel that those who are generous enough to give them free access to online resources deserve to be taken advantage of.

Here's an example of the sort of lowlife that can hurt your Web community. In the old days, it was pretty common to share a folder on the Web through anonymous FTP. A visitor could share files with other visitors by uploading it to the shared folder.

Today, allowing anonymous visitors to write files to your Web server is considered suicide. Opportunists troll the Web for servers with this vulnerability. Then they upload gigabytes and gigabytes of junk. We've seen it happen to two of our customers, and the files can be very difficult to remove once they are in place, due to some clever file naming strategies.

If you have used a public bulletin board or newsgroup, perhaps at your favorite portal site, you've probably had to waste your time wading through endless defamatory, rude, and bigoted diatribes. These are posted by loonies who use the service as their personal soapbox.

After a while, you get a few of these folks virtually yelling at each other online, and the discussion group, blog, or bulletin board becomes too irritating to use. Most portal sites have had to adopt a registration requirement so they can control who has access to the service and cut off participants who become obnoxious. If this kind of thing happens on your site, it can damage your company's image and drive customers away. On our own forum, we've had to spend quite a bit of time "locking it down" to keep out spam and other riff raff. We also turned off comments in our blog because it just wasn't worth the aggravation of wading through the comment spam.

The only way to avoid these problems is to make sure that the public is never allowed to provide content that appears directly on your Web site. The most common way to restrict access is to put all facilities that accept visitor input behind a login screen.

You then give your customers a login name and password, which gives them access to the restricted areas. When they visit your site, they must log in before they can do anything. Although this approach creates more work for you and your visitors, it can also make the customer feel more special. You can rest a little easier, knowing that the Unibomber can't post his manifesto to your Web site without your knowledge.

For even more control, you can let registered users post information, but not allow the information to appear on your site until you review it and accept it. For a business Web site, it often isn't necessary to go to this extreme. After all, these visitors are your customers. They have their own image to protect as well as a business relationship with you that presumably is valuable to them. You don't bite the hand that gives you free access to support on the Web!

Web site security measures are meant to deal with Internet vandals, not genuine visitors. Unfortunately, as long as the vandals are out there, you must be prepared to protect your site from them! And now, more and more of the problems come from automated "bots" so you aren't even dealing with living vandals, but the products of their nefarious programs.

Courtesy is Contagious

Here at Logical Expressions we have learned a great deal about how to improve our relationships with all our business contacts. These tips apply to any business, large or small, Internet-based or traditional. You've probably heard most of them before, but I'm going to add a personal slant on how they've affected us.

- Get agreements in writing. We aren't really talking about hiring a lawyer to write up a long contract, although that is certainly appropriate when big money is involved. But you should write down the scope of work and the cost of that work. That way, you and your customer have something to refer to later.

  People forget, and, sadly, some people try to get sneaky. In either case, you don't want the "but I thought you said" conversation that inevitably results. Under these circumstances, collecting payments in arrears becomes virtually impossible. Trust us on this, we know.

- Pay your bills on time. If you are unable to make payment in full, contact the vendor and ask for terms. If you don't pay and say nothing about it, the vendor thinks you are blowing them off and that you never intend to pay. My feelings are, if you can't pay for it, don't ask for it in the first place.

  Our business is increasingly moving to a pay-in-advance scheme to avoid the collection hassles. I'm astounded at how many businesses are willing to destroy their relationship with us by failing to pay for the work we've already completed for them. I'm not talking about unsatisfied customers, either.

- Reward your best customers. If you have customers who regularly pay on time and are easy to work with, reward them with special discounts. Be sure to thank them for their diligence. These customers are the few diamonds in a sea of coal.

  On the other hand, you can make doing business with dud customers worthwhile by increasing the rate you charge them. We call this the "aggravation surcharge." Don't be mistaken: managing difficult customers costs you extra time and money. Make them pay for it. Don't worry too much about losing these customers. You want to cultivate your best customers. Let the competition struggle with the duds.

- Plan ahead to avoid fire-fighting mode. Planning ahead has pretty much gone out the window. The result is a struggling economy weighed down with workers who don't want to work and managers who don't want to manage. Don't be one of them. We need to stop crying about today and start dreaming of what we want for tomorrow. Set some goals and work toward them. Sitting around and waiting for the next crisis is demoralizing and counterproductive.

- Respond to communications. We are frequently frustrated by the lack of response to voice mail and email messages. Sure, we understand that people are busy fighting fires or that they may just be out of the office. But letting a message go for days with absolutely no response is insulting.

You can go a long way toward establishing good will with your customers and business partners by simply being courteous enough to respond (however briefly) to their communications.

Learn to Delegate and Automate

We talked a bit about outsourcing in the section on how to hire a Web developer, but we'd like to extend this concept a little further. After all, no business is an island. When you are feeling overwhelmed it may be a sign that it's time to delegate.

After all, as a business owner, you need to consider what your time is worth. It's probably not what you think. Suppose you are hoping to put up a Web site and start a new business on the side. You work at a fast food joint during the day for $7.50 an hour, so you probably think your time is worth $7.50 an hour. You can't imagine paying some Web designer $30/hour to create a page for you.

We'd like you to look at it a different way. As we've said before, planning and setting goals are important. You can't reach a goal if you never set it in the first place.

So with that in mind, suppose you want to make $50,000 in sales from your Web site in the next year. If your past sales from January through March are $1,000/month, you aren't going to make it. You've got only 8 months to make $47,000. So if you divide $47,000 by 8, you need to make $5,875 each month.

Now let's look at how much time you have to make that $5,875. Most people aren't really productive 8 hours/day. And if you're working part time, you may have a lot less time than that. Suppose you allocate 4 hours/day 5 days a week. That's 20 hours, multiplied by 4 weeks or 80 hours. Divide $5,875 by 80 and you see that your real hourly rate is $73.

Now NOT outsourcing looks kind of stupid doesn't it?

Okay, maybe if you're working at the fast food joint, you don't have $30/hour to pay a Web developer. In that case, you need to learn how to create sites yourself. In business, there's a trade-off between time and money. If you have money, you can pay someone to do the things you don't have time to do. But if you don't have money and need to do a task yourself, accept the reality that it will take you more time to create the site than it would a pro.

Once you've thought about your hourly rate, you can see why automating your business systems is so important. For example, some people try to keep track of email newsletter subscribes and unsubscribes in their personal email program. This type of thing is not a good use of your time. You are spending your $73 hourly rate doing something that could be automated by software. If you spend $20/month on an ezine service that has this feature built-in, you just gave your business back some of your valuable time!

Look for opportunities to automate and streamline your business. If you are sitting there thinking, "wow, what a bunch of busywork; why am I doing this?" you shouldn't be!

Embrace Failure

In the world of business, no one ever talks about failure, which is stupid. Realistically, businesses fail all the time, partly because the owners were too shy or embarrassed to ask for help.

Realistically, you learn from your mistakes. Despite what Internet gurus will tell you, no marketing technique is a surefire winner. The best-marketed products can still fail. Sometimes you are just in the wrong place at the wrong time.

For example, when we were publishing our magazine, we spent a lot of time setting up and sending out a huge direct marketing mailing. We mailed it on September 10, 2001. Needless to say, we got a zero percent response rate. You can't account for every variable. Sometimes things happen that are completely out of your control.

But with that said, on the Internet, you have a tremendous opportunity to see the results of your efforts. You try a marketing approach and you can see the results of it just by checking your stats. When something doesn't work, try something else. Be bold and don't do what everyone else is doing.

A Few Final Tips

By now you have a good idea of what it takes to create a great business Web site. You've got plenty of ideas and options to consider! That's why proper planning is extremely important.

Before you build even one Web page, stop and do your homework. Visualize what you want your site to look like. Think about the message you want it to convey. Go back to the beginning of this book, and read about Web site goals and bubble diagrams.

Here are a few final tips:

- Talk to your existing customers. What would they like to see on your Web site? How can they use it to save time? How can they use it to save money? How can they use it to speed up the process of doing business with you?

- Get expert help. Although you can try to do the job yourself or assign the task to one of your employees, you will not get professional results unless you hire a professional. Don't try to build a house if you aren't a carpenter.

- Find a designer/developer with whom you are compatible. Once you figure out what you want, make sure you find someone who can give it to you! If you have difficulty communicating what you need, your project will be a struggle from start to finish. If the designer/developer doesn't seem to get it, move on.

- Research your options. Surf the Web and locate sites with features you like and don't like. Write them down. The more examples you can give your designer, the better. Remember the trade-offs discussed earlier between speed and flash.

- Plan, plan, plan. We'll say it one last time: the more planning you do up front, the more likely your project will succeed. Diving straight in will waste your money. Make sure you know what you are going to do before you start doing it.

Ready? Now, go forth and e-transact!

Business Resources

Online sites with business management articles and sites for finding people to help you.

Business Information

- All Business - http://www.allbusiness.com/

- FindLaw Legal Information - http://www.findlaw.com

- Forbes Magazine - http://www.forbes.com

- BusinessWeek magazine - http://www.businessweek.com

- SmartBiz - http://www.smartbiz.com

- Tax Information for Businesses - http://www.irs.gov/businesses/

Freelance/Job Sites

- Guru - http://www.guru.com

- Elance - http://www.elance.com

- RentaCoder - http://www.rentacoder.com

- SoloGig - http://www.sologig.com

- Monster - http://www.monster.com

- CareerBuilder - http://www.careerbuilder.com

Glossary

404 Error: The error message you get when a visitor lands on a Web site page that isn't available. It generally is because of a broken link or deleted page.

Above the Fold: The part of a Web page that is visible on screen without scrolling vertically.

Affiliate Program: A program that pays a commission to Web sites that drive visitors to another site. The business running the affiliate program may pay an affiliate for clicks, leads, or sales.

Alternate Text/Alt Text: Text you add to graphics or objects that appear while pictures are loading into a Web page.

Ajax: Asynchronous JavaScript and XML. With Ajax, Web browsers can communicate with the Web server without having to refresh the entire Web page each time.

Animation: Visual effects you can add to a Web page using GIF animation or Flash.

ASP: 1. Application Service Provider. A company that provides a service that runs as hosted software on their Web server for a monthly fee.
2. Active Server Pages: A technology that generates Web pages dynamically, which is used most often on Microsoft Windows servers.

Aspect Ratio: The relationship between the height and width of an image. If you maintain an object's aspect ratio as you resize it, the image does not become distorted.

Attachment: A file you include with an email message.

Autoresponder: An email service that automatically responds to an email sent to it by sending out an automatic reply. A "sequential" autoresponder sends out a series of replies at specified intervals.

Banner Ad: An image-based advertisement that is placed on a Web site encouraging people to click the link to take them to the advertiser's site.

BBS/Bulletin Board Service: See "Newsgroup"

Blog: A date-based Web site where people can add comments.

Bitmap: An image made up of a collection of dots. Scanned images and certain image formats such as .JPG and .GIF are bitmap files.

Bold: A version of a typeface in which the letters appear with heavier or thicker lines.

Browser: A software program used to view Web pages. Microsoft Internet Explorer and Mozilla Firefox are two examples of browsers.

Browser-Safe Color: One of the 216 common colors that are shared across browsers, operating systems, and computer platforms.

Cache: A temporary storage location on your hard disk used to store information that will be needed again. Browsers have a cache so that they can store elements of frequently accessed pages, and load them more quickly. Sometimes it is necessary to "clear" or "empty" the cache if the browser is storing outdated information.

CGI: Common Gateway Interface. A scripting language used on Web servers that is often used to process form data. CGI programs are often stored in a folder called Cgi-Bin.

Chat: An online service that lets people have text-based conversations in real-time.

Certificate Authority: A certificate authority is an organization that has been authorized to sell SSL certificates.

Comp: Comp is short for "composition." A Web site comp is a graphic image that is basically a sample picture of what the site will look like. Web graphic designers often use comps to demonstrate the look of the site without committing the design to HTML, which is usually much harder to modify.

Cookie: A tiny file that is sent to the server by your browser, generally to store your preferences or settings between browser sessions. (Sites that welcome you back by name use cookies to store this information.)

Crawler: See "Spider"

Cyberspace: Another term for the Internet. The term was originally coined by author William Gibson in his novel *Neuromancer*.

Domain Email Account: This is an email account that uses the domain name you registered for your Web site. For example, support@MyDomain.com.

Domain Name: A domain name is the name you select to represent your business on the Internet. For example, Logical Expressions, Inc. uses the domain name LogicalExpressions.com.

Domain Registrar: A domain registrar is a company that is authorized to sell and register domain names. For the best pricing and service, LEI recommends GoDaddy. com.

Download: To transfer information from the Internet "down" to your computer. (See also "Upload")

DNS Server: A DNS server routes requests for your domain name to the correct location in the Internet. When you browse to a specific domain, like www.MyDomain. com, DNS servers route the request to the Web server that hosts your Web site.

Ecommerce: The practice of buying and selling over the Internet.

Email: Electronic Mail. A system allowing you to send messages from one computer to another over some kind of communications network, such as a local area network, online service, or the Internet. Or the text or HTML message itself that is sent from one computer to another over the Internet. An "email client" is software used to send and receive email. (See also "Web Mail")

Ezine: A newsletter or other periodic publication sent by email. The word is a shortened form of "electronic magazine."

FAQ: Frequently Asked Questions. A page on a Web site or other document that answers the most common questions on a particular subject.

Flame: To send a nasty email. Or the term for the nasty email itself.

Font: The characters of a given type size in a given typeface and style such as 10 point Times New Roman Italic. Often used interchangeably with typeface, typestyle, or type family.

Forum: See "Newsgroup"

FTP: FTP stands for File Transfer Protocol. Your Web developer uses FTP to transfer files to and from your Web server.

GIF: Graphic Interchange Format. A type of graphic file format that is often used for files being placed on Web pages that will be viewed over the World Wide Web. GIF files are saved with a .GIF extension.

Hit: In the context of Web site statistics, a request to the Web server to provide a particular file. A single visitor to a Web site can cause many "hits," especially on a page that uses a lot of graphics because downloading each graphic counts as a hit.

Home Page: The opening page of a Web site, often default.htm, default.html, index. htm, or index.html.

Hosting Company: A hosting company (or simply "host") is an organization that operates Web servers and mail servers connected to the Internet through high-speed lines. For a fee, a hosting company sets up your Web site and email accounts on their servers so you can take advantage of their high-speed access and server maintenance expertise.

HTML: HyperText Markup Language. HTML is a page description language that tells your Web browser how to render a Web page.

HTTP/HTTPS: HyperText Transport Protocol. The communication rules that make it possible to exchange files over the World Wide Web. HTTPS stands for HTTP over SSL or HyperText Transport Protocol Secure, which enables the secure transmission of Web pages. It is extremely important to secure pages whenever sensitive or financial information is being transferred, such as banking and ecommerce applications. (See also "SSL")

Hyperlink: A graphic or underlined text that you click to jump to another point in a presentation, another file, or a location on the World Wide Web.

Image Map: An image that has clickable links in it to take the visitor to different pages.

Internet: A communications network in which collections of computer networks and gateways are connected using a protocol called TCP/IP. Sending and receiving email and accessing the World Wide Web are common uses of the Internet.

Intranet: A communications network set up within an organization that uses a similar setup and protocols as the Internet.

ISP: Internet Service Provider. A company that sells individuals or companies an Internet connection so they can get online. Your computer is connected to the Internet through your ISP.

Italic: A version of a typeface in which the letters appear slanted.

Keywords: Descriptive terms in Web page meta tags used by search engines. Also significant terms within the text of Web pages that search engines use to determine content.

JavaScript/Java: A language used for scripts on Web pages. JavaScript is a simplified version of Java used for scripting that doesn't have to be compiled. Sometimes the term Java is (erroneously) used interchangeably with JavaScript. JavaScript actually is a subset of the Java programming language.

JPEG: Joint Photographic Experts Group. A JPEG file (often having a .jpg extension) is a bitmap image that has been compressed to minimize space. The file format is named after the standards committee that developed it.

List Server: Software that manages an email mailing list or discussion group.

Meta Tag: An HTML tag that provides information about a Web page. The most common meta tags are descriptions and keywords, which some search engines use to index the page. Meta tags are not visible to Web page visitors.

Merchant Account: A merchant account is a special bank account that is designed to accept credit card and e-check transactions through the electronic financial network. The merchant account can often be tied to your regular business checking account.

Payment Gateway: A payment gateway is what lets your Web site collect money from customers while you do other things. When a customer places an order on your Web site, your shopping cart software submits the transaction to the payment gateway for authorization. The payment gateway communicates with the appropriate financial networks to verify that the customer is allowed to make the purchase. The payment gateway also queues up the transactions for a nightly batch settlement.

Podcast: A method of publishing sound files to the Internet that allows people to receive them through a feed. (See "RSS")

Newsgroup: A discussion group related to a particular topic. Often used interchangeably with forum or bulletin board. Historically, newsgroups were within the USENET system, although now the term newsgroup is used as more of a generic term for a discussion group.

Opt-in/Opt-out: Opt-in is the process by which a subscriber requests to receive information or an ezine via email from a company. The converse is opt-out, where people are signed up automatically and have to specifically request *not* to receive information.

Newbie: Someone who is new to a computing subject, such as using the Internet.

RGB: Red, Green, Blue. The color model in which colors are made up of different values of the component colors red, green and blue. Because RGB is used by computer monitors, it is used to specify colors that will be viewed over the Internet.

RSS: Rich Site Summary or Really Simple Syndication. Used to syndicate content to other sites or notify people automatically when a site is updated.

Script: Programming code inserted into a Web page or on a server to add dynamic features.

Server: A computer running special software that is connected to the Internet. Depending on the software, servers may "serve" Web pages (Web server), email (mail server), and other types of data.

Signature: A block of text at the bottom of an email identifying the sender. A signature often also includes promotional information and/or Web site links.

Site: See "Web Site"

Shopping Cart Software: When you set up an ecommerce site, you need software that displays the products in your product catalog, lets your customers add items to a virtual shopping basket, and then accepts electronic payment from the customer at checkout. The software also includes an administration interface that you can use to set up your product catalog and configure shipping and payment options. That software is commonly called shopping cart software, although it does much more.

Spam: Unsolicited email that is broadcast to people who did not ask to receive it.

Spider: Spiders (or crawlers) are software that search engines use to find pages on the Internet. The program "crawls" from page to page, adding pages into the search engine index.

SSL: Secured Sockets Layer. This protocol is what makes your Internet transactions secure. It has two primary functions: It verifies that you are who you say you are, and it encrypts all of the data that goes back and forth between the visitor's browser and your Web site. Without SSL, it is possible for Internet hackers to capture credit card numbers and other sensitive information as it flows between the browser and your site.

SSL Certificate: An SSL certificate is a file that associates your domain name with a specific Web server. You need an SSL certificate in order to use the SSL protocol that encrypts information between your customer's Web browser and your Web site. You must buy a certificate from an authorized certificate authority using information you get from your hosting company.

Subscribe: To request to receive information by email, such as an ezine or autoresponder sequence. To stop receiving information, you "unsubscribe."

Thread: In a discussion group or forum, the initial posting and the various sequence of responses that follow it.

Thumbnail: A small version of an image used on a Web site to keep the page size smaller. Often when you click the thumbnail, a larger version of the image is displayed.

Upload: To transfer information from your computer "up" to the Internet, such as uploading files to your Web site. (See also "Download")

Unsubscribe: See "Subscribe"

URL: Uniform Resource Locator. The address of a Web page or other destination on the Internet. You type a URL, such as www.logicalexpressions.com into your browser's address bar.

Web/World Wide Web/WWW: One part of the Internet that is made up of Web pages that are viewed using a browser. It is the network of servers that are linked together and use HTTP to transfer pages and files.

Web Mail: Sending and receiving email through a browser instead of through an email client. (See also "Email")

Web Site: A group of related Web pages that generally are linked together. Also refers to the files stored in a particular location on a Web server that is connected to the Internet. The Web site is generally owned or maintained by the person or company that also owns the domain name.

Web Server: See "Server."

XML: Extensible Markup Language. A system for defining data formats. On the Web, often used in conjunction with RSS feeds because RSS feeds use XML to transmit the data.

Index

About
Logical Expressions, Inc.

About LEI

Logical Expressions, Inc. is a company that creates books, software, and online publications. The company was formed in California in 1994 by Susan Daffron and James Byrd. The couple moved themselves, the company, and their cats to Idaho in 1996 to escape the smog and freeways of Southern California city life.

From their main office in a log home in the middle of a forest, the company develops software and publications and consults with clients throughout the United States. Their most recent software release is a writing and creativity program called IdeaWeaver (http://www.IdeaWeaverSoftware.com).

In addition to owning ecommerce sites, they publish a weekly computer tips ezine called Logical Tips (http://www.Logical Tips.com), a pet care ezine called Pet Tails (http://www.pet-tails.com), a newsletter about Sandpoint, Idaho called the Sandpoint Insider (http://www.sandpointinsider.com), and an online Computer Magazine called Computor Companion (http://www.ComputorCompanion.com).

Contacts:
Susan Daffron, President, Logical Expressions, Inc.
Phone: 208-265-6147
Email: sdaffron@logicalexpressions.com

James Byrd, Vice President, Logical Expressions, Inc.
Phone: 208-265-3646
Email: jhbyrd@logicalexpressions.com

LEI Web site
http://www.logicalexpressions.com

Share Web Business Success with a Friend

If you like this book, share it with your friends!

Order Form

Please send me:

Qty	Title	Price	Total
	Web Business Success	$29.95	
	Shipping & Handling - $4.50 for first book, $1.00 for each additional book for US Priority Mail within the U.S.*		

____ Check enclosed with order

____ Please charge my credit card   [   ] Visa   [   ] Master Card

Number: _____

Name on Card: _____ Exp. Date: _____

Buyer's Name:_____

Buyer's Address: _____

Shipping Address (if different):_____

_____

Please fax to 208-265-0956 or mail order form with your payment to:

Logical Expressions, Inc.
311 Fox Glen Rd.
Sandpoint, ID 83864

*   *Please contact us for more information on orders mailed outside of the U.S. (Our number is 208-265-6147)*

Printed in the United States
100633LV00002B/82/A

9 780974 924502